The Ultimate Guide to Successful Corporate Finance Job Interviewing

M. L. Miller

Published by SoaringME Publishing

ISBN-13: 978-1-956874-22-8

CONTENTS

Preface

Dear Reader,

If you're seeking to enhance your interview prowess and secure your ideal job or advancement opportunity, you've come to the right place. My path to authoring this book began in 1997 when I approached a recruiting firm in search of a finance job. Having studied finance, I envisioned a long career in the field. However, fate led me to work for the firm, under its owner Larry, where I immersed myself in the world of talent acquisition, recruiting, and interviewing. With the benefit of Larry's extensive experience spanning over two decades and my own acquired skills, I facilitated hundreds of hires and contributed to significant growth for numerous organizations.

Throughout the years, I've recruited for a wide array of roles, including finance, and collaborated with both large and small companies. This experience has granted me invaluable insights into the intricacies of employer hiring processes and successful strategies. In 2009, my focus shifted to executive recruiting, yet I continued to field requests for assistance from individuals at the onset of their careers. Consequently, I established SoaringME, a company dedicated to helping candidates refine their interviewing abilities.

After considerable contemplation, I've at last penned this book to impart the knowledge I've gained about effective interviewing. The guidance in this book begins once you've secured an interview, thanks to your compelling resume, professional social media presence, or networking efforts. My aim is to equip you with everything I lacked back in 1997, empowering you to excel in interviews and attain the job or promotion you desire. This book includes all the information from my other book *SoaringME The Ultimate Guide to Successful Job Interviewing*, with additional content specifically geared towards excelling in corporate finance interviews.

Best of luck, and I hope that you get the job or promotion that you're going for!

M. L. Miller

Founder, SoaringME

If you enjoy this book, please give it a review.

Visit

for additional resources.

Introduction

In *SoaringME The Ultimate Guide to Successful Corporate Finance Job Interviewing,* the insights and advice will boost your chances of success in any job interview process, particularly for corporate finance roles such as Financial Analyst, Financial Reporting Analyst, Treasury Analyst, Operations Analyst, BD Analyst, Pricing Analyst, FP&A, Risk Management, Strategic Finance, Corporate Development/M&A, Asset Management, Treasury, Investor Relations, and CFO positions.

For employers, recruiting, hiring, and training new employees is a costly and time-consuming process. As a result, companies have developed hiring processes that increase their ability to find the best match for the job and the organization. These processes act as a test, and you need to pass it to receive an offer of employment.

Interviewing can be challenging and anxiety-inducing for many candidates. Spending a good amount of time preparing for the interviews is critical to maximizing your success rate and reducing any anxiety. The best-prepared candidates interview more successfully because they feel confident during their interviews, leading to stronger answers to questions and a better overall impression.

Interview questions are designed to uncover information that the employer needs to decide who the best fit for the job is. Your primary objective during this process is to demonstrate through your answers and actions that you are the best match to the ideal profile of who they want to hire. You also want to gather information about the employer, the job, expectations, company culture, and compensation so that you can make an informed decision on whether this opportunity is a good fit for you.

This book will teach you what the people who will be grading your test are looking for and what the most successful candidates have done. It's important to note that none of the following advice is meant for you to be dishonest in your interviews or try to be someone you're not. The Ultimate Guide to Successful Corporate Finance Job Interviewing will help you maximize your chances of getting your dream job by focusing your answers on demonstrating the value you will bring to the position that you're interviewing for.

On average, Americans change jobs 12 times in their career, meaning people will go through the interview process once every three to four years. Even candidates with a lot of career experience often fail in an interview process simply because it's not something they do that often, and it's unfamiliar. This lack of familiarity can result in candidates receiving unexpected questions and making mistakes.

Confident candidates perform better in job interviews than nervous ones do. To build your confidence, do your research, organize ahead of time, practice answering interview questions, and reverse roles to ask those questions of somebody else so that you understand the interviewers' point of view. Become familiar with what you will encounter, and you will lessen or eliminate nervousness by avoiding surprises. While in the interview, focus on your skills and traits that match the profile and don't focus on the outcome.

In this book, I've included chapters on questions for you to ask employers and employer red flags to watch out for. Remember that not all companies have figured out their hiring process, and that's okay. The Ultimate Guide to Successful Corporate Finance Job Interviewing will help you navigate any interview process with confidence and ease.

Corporate Finance Careers

Corporate finance is a dynamic and exciting field that provides numerous opportunities for growth and development. The entry-level roles in corporate finance include financial analyst, financial reporting analyst, treasury analyst, operations analyst, BD/M&A analyst, pricing analyst, and FP&A analyst. These professionals are tasked with analyzing financial data and creating financial models to help businesses make informed decisions. As they gain more experience, corporate finance professionals can progress to mid-level roles such as risk management, strategic finance, corporate development/M&A, asset management, and treasury.

These mid-level roles require a higher level of responsibility for the financial health and success of the organization. In these positions, professionals are responsible for managing risk, developing financial strategies, and executing corporate transactions such as mergers and acquisitions. They play a critical role in the management and growth of a company by providing financial analysis and strategic planning.

More senior and executive-level roles in corporate finance include Strategic Finance Managers, Corporate Development/M&A Managers, Asset Management Managers, Treasury Managers, Investor Relations Managers, and ultimately, CFOs. These roles involve more strategic decision-making and a higher level of responsibility for the financial health and success of the organization. In these positions, professionals are responsible for communicating financial information to shareholders and investors and overseeing the company's financial operations.

One of the great things about a career in corporate finance is the variety of roles and opportunities available. The demand for skilled corporate finance professionals is high, meaning that there are plenty of job opportunities and room for growth. Additionally, a career in corporate finance can be quite lucrative as professionals progress into more senior roles. The potential for high earnings, coupled with the opportunity for bonuses and other performance-based incentives, can make a career in corporate finance quite appealing.

A career in corporate finance is a great choice for individuals with an interest in finance and a talent for strategic thinking and decision-making. The skills and experience gained in corporate finance are highly transferable, making it possible for professionals to transition into other areas of finance or business. It offers opportunities for growth and advancement, as well as competitive salaries and benefits. Corporate finance is a challenging and rewarding path for individuals interested in the world of finance and business.

Understanding What Recruiters and Hiring Managers are Looking For

To succeed in any interview process, it is vital to have a comprehensive understanding of what the interviewers are seeking. The foundation of this success lies in spending ample time to grasp as much detail as possible about the ideal profile being sought.

When a company decides to create a new job, it's because they have a need in their organization, and if they find the right person, the company will be more successful. To identify the ideal candidate, companies start with outlining the duties required for the role and develop a profile of the best-suited employee. Depending on the organization's size, the hiring manager, Human Resources, Talent Acquisition, upper management, or a combination of these may create this profile. The profile can be influenced by the hiring manager's personal preferences, the team's current makeup, or the previous employee's qualities.

The ideal candidate's profile comprises hard skills, soft skills, and personality traits, and while these traits vary slightly from company to company, most employers seek some specific traits in a new employee. These traits might not even be mentioned in the job advertisement, but interviewers still evaluate candidates on them. In the chapter on *How to Stand Out from Others*, we cover how understanding these hidden traits can provide an edge over other candidates.

Here are the eleven most common universal traits that interviewers are seeking.

1. Effective communication skills.
2. Passion for that work.
3. Self-motivated.
4. Works well with others.
5. Competent.
6. Ability to take responsibility for work and mistakes.
7. Good problem-solving skills.
8. Honest.
9. Ability to listen.

10. Nice to work with.

11. Reliable.

To identify the perfect candidate for a job, companies typically have a list of desired qualities and attributes, including educational background, training, experience, and personality traits. These may consist of a college degree, specific major, certifications, industry experience, knowledge of relevant software programs or programming languages, and other tools required for the role. The ideal candidate's personality may be characterized by being coachable, drive for future advancement, good teamwork skills, or ability to work independently.

The interview process is a series of steps designed to assess how well a candidate matches this ideal person, with the goal of eliminating candidates who are not a good fit. The job advertisement, interview questions, and final decision on who to offer the job to are all based on this profile.

Understanding the profile for a job is critical to success, as every company has a preconceived notion of the person they want to hire. This profile can be divided into two sides: the skills or experience side and the personality or compatibility with the company culture side. By having a solid grasp of this profile, you can position yourself as the best-suited candidate and increase your chances of securing the job.

Here are the best steps to understanding the ideal profile for a specific job.

1.   Research 10-20 job ads for similar jobs. Make a list of the duties required and desired attributes listed in all these advertisements.

2.   Research the backgrounds of employees who are currently in similar roles. Look at the 10-20 LinkedIn profiles and the background they had before being hired for a job like the one you want.

3.   Ask contacts in your professional network what they think makes people successful in that job, or if they know what type of candidate that company prefers to hire for that type of role.

4.   Compile the attributes that repeatedly show up in your research. This is a great starting point for understanding what the interviewers are going to evaluate you against.

To succeed in an interview, it's crucial to understand the list of required and desired attributes listed in the job advertisement. These traits are usually listed in descending order of importance, and understanding them is crucial to your success. The *COMPANION WORKBOOK The Ultimate Guide to Successful Job Interviewing* includes exercises that can help you understand the job profile, which may include many unwritten desired traits that you'll need to research.

It's important to note that job profiles usually represent a wish list for the hiring manager, not an absolute minimum. If you match 60% or more of the job profile, you should apply for the job. Some managers may take a chance on a candidate who only possesses 60-70% of the desired skills if they fit the ideal personality and are trainable on the rest. However, it's unlikely that you'll receive job offers in most cases where you're only a 60-70% match, and you may not even be interviewed.

During the interview, make sure to highlight areas in your background that relate to the job profile and avoid providing irrelevant information. Your resume should show the overlap you have with the ideal profile, and you should provide more detailed answers during the interview. For example, a nurse or therapist job profile may include experience working with elderly patients, so you should highlight your experience in this area.

Understanding the ideal profile is essential, as demonstrated by a Vice President candidate I worked with who didn't advance after the first interview. Despite having the necessary education and skillset, the candidate displayed hesitation in making decisions and asking questions during the interview with the startup employer. The role called for an individual who could take charge, be assertive, and propel projects forward. This candidate's prior experience with large corporations, where they functioned as a mere cog in the wheel, was a better fit for their personality which did not align with the desired personality traits. It's crucial to note that comprehending the ideal profile does not imply pretending to be someone else, but rather showcasing how you meet the requirements through your conduct and responses during the interview process.

Corporate Finance Candidate Profiles

The typical background profile for corporate finance job candidates, including roles like Financial Analyst, Financial Reporting Analyst, Treasury Analyst, Operations Analyst, BD Analyst, Pricing Analyst, FP&A, Risk Management, Strategic Finance, Corporate Development/M&A, Asset Management, Treasury, Investor Relations, and CFC, usually consists of the following elements:

1. Education: A bachelor's degree in finance, accounting, economics, or a related field is generally required. For more advanced positions or specific roles like Risk Management or Corporate Development, a master's degree in finance, MBA, or another relevant advanced degree may be preferred or required.

2. Professional certifications: Candidates may hold certifications such as Chartered Financial Analyst (CFA),

Certified Public Accountant (CPA), Certified Treasury Professional (CTP), Financial Risk Manager (FRM), or others that are relevant to their specific role.

3. Technical skills: Proficiency in financial analysis, forecasting, modeling, and knowledge of accounting principles is essential. Additionally, candidates should be adept at using financial software and tools like Microsoft Excel, financial reporting systems, and enterprise resource planning (ERP) systems.

4. Work experience: Depending on the role, candidates may have varying levels of experience in corporate finance, financial analysis, treasury, risk management, or related fields. Entry-level positions may require internships or 1-2 years of experience, while senior roles or specialized positions like CFOs usually necessitate 10+ years of experience and a track record of success in finance leadership.

5. Soft skills: Corporate finance professionals should possess strong analytical, problem-solving, communication, and interpersonal skills. They should also be detail-oriented, able to work under pressure, manage multiple tasks, and adapt to rapidly changing business environments.

6. Industry knowledge: Some roles may require specific industry knowledge, especially if they are in highly regulated or specialized industries. Familiarity with relevant regulations, industry trends, and competitive landscapes can be advantageous.

7. Networking and affiliations: Active participation in professional organizations or industry groups, as well as a well-established professional network, can be beneficial for career growth and job opportunities.

Please note that the background profile for each role may vary depending on the company's requirements, size, and industry. It is essential to tailor your qualifications and skills to the specific job description and requirements of the position you are targeting.

How You Will be Evaluated

Preparation is essential for a successful interview. Candidates who don't prepare are viewed as less professional and less interested, leading to fears of underperformance and short tenures if hired. The most successful candidates plan, understand the employer's ideal profile, organize their thoughts and memories, and relate their skills, experience, and traits to that profile.

Employers use the ideal profile to develop an interview process that evaluates candidates' suitability for the position. Interviewers may be experienced enough to ask individual questions, while others may use an interview packet. To understand what interviewers are seeking in your answers, imagine yourself as the interviewer looking for the ideal profile.

For example, imagine you're interviewing candidates for the Director or Senior Director of Regulatory Affairs role in a biotech company. Apply this same process to whatever job you're interviewing for to prepare for a successful interview.

Here is part of the job advertisement that explains the ideal profile that we're looking for:

Primary responsibilities include:

- Participates with key stakeholders to formulate regulatory strategies.
- Plan and manage integration of multidisciplinary regulatory programs into the project team development plans for all assigned projects.
- Lead the planning of and conduct meetings with regulatory agencies as appropriate. May represent the company at regulatory agency meetings as appropriate.
- Perform regulatory intelligence activities to keep current on the regulatory environment and competitive products.
- Provide the company with current and proposed regulatory and scientific issues.
- Manage and review safety reports and submissions.

Education and Skills Requirements:

- Demonstrated knowledge of the drug development process is essential.
- Knowledge of laws and regulations affecting the pharmaceutical industry and regulatory experience.
- Must have prior experience working with the FDA or EMA.
- Experience in successful NDA, BLA or MAA filings is essential.
- Prior management experience preferred. Must demonstrate the ability to work through others.
- Highly organized, with attention to detail.
- Advanced scientific degree preferred. B.A. or B.S. or higher degree(s) in the sciences, or health-related field minimum, with 7+ years of regulatory experience (Director) and 10+ years of regulatory experience (Sr. Director.) Demonstrates personal leadership and collaboration skills.
- Travel up to 25%.

To prepare for an interview, imagine yourself as one of the interviewers. I will provide you with an interview packet that contains a list of traits we are looking for in the ideal candidate and ten to twenty different questions for each trait. These questions are designed to assess the candidate's skills or experience and evaluate their proficiency in that area.

For instance, the packet for the Director or Senior Director of Regulatory Affairs role in a biotech company might include traits like regulatory strategy, leadership, communication skills, and attention to detail. Under each trait, the packet will provide questions that will help evaluate the candidate's abilities and how they fit the ideal profile.

By practicing this mental exercise, you can anticipate the type of questions that interviewers may ask and prepare accordingly. This way, you'll be better equipped to demonstrate how you match the ideal profile during the interview and improve your chances of success.

"Prior management experience preferred. Must demonstrate the ability to work through others." As you prepare to interview these candidates, here is how your packet questions might look for the management experience that we are looking for:

Management experience:

Q1: How do you give feedback to others, and how do you hold them accountable?

Q2: Tell me about a project that you led. What made it successful?

Q3: How do you manage stress among team members?

Q3: Tell me about a time that you influenced other team members on a project. How did that work out?

Q4: Describe to me a time when you managed somebody who was struggling.

Q5: How do you plan for your team members' professional development?

Q6: How do you handle conflict between team members?

Q7: Tell me about a time when you had to let a team member go. Why? How did they take it?

Q8: How do you motivate people?

Q9: How have you successfully delegated to others?

Q10: What is your biggest management weakness?

During the interview process, each interviewer will usually be assigned three to five traits to evaluate in the candidate. The interview packet contains a list of ten to twenty questions for each trait, and each interviewer will choose one question to ask the candidate. There may be some overlap where multiple interviewers evaluate the same skill, and the candidate's resume may affect the questions asked.

In addition to hard skills, interviewers are also evaluating personality fit and how long it will take the candidate to become a highly contributing member of the team. After all interviews are completed, interviewers will compare candidates in a feedback meeting and may develop a favorite candidate to advocate for. Candidates who create multiple advocates will have a higher chance of getting the job offer.

To succeed in the interview process, prepare well for each interview, regardless of the interviewer. Get into a relaxed, professional, and likable frame of mind to make a good impression. By doing so, you can create advocates and increase your chances of securing the job.

This is how your answers are analyzed.

As a candidate, every answer you give in an interview must meet the minimum credibility standard set by each interviewer. For example, taking credit for territory rankings or success in a sales position after just three months may not be credible if the typical sales cycle is six to nine months. Similarly, claiming to be downsized when your former company is hiring and expanding will also harm your credibility. Only credible answers will increase the strength of your candidacy.

Interviewers prioritize the strength of a candidate's answers when evaluating feedback and making hiring decisions. A strong answer leaves the interviewer with confidence that you could be a good employee, and the strength of your answer is directly related to the impression you leave with the interviewer. The hierarchy of impressiveness may vary depending on the type of interview questions and the industry or sector of the job.

Therefore, when preparing for an interview, pay special attention to how impressive your answers are likely to be. This will help you organize your thoughts and memories in a way that highlights your strengths and presents you as a strong candidate.

Hierarchy of impressiveness for interview answers.
1. Verifiable accomplishments. (i.e., awards, recognition, publications, or rankings.)
2. Accomplishments that are harder to verify.
3. Good success stories that directly relate to the job.
4. A good example of past success that indirectly relates to the job.
5. An example that demonstrates a personality trait that fits the profile.
6. Demonstrating personality traits during interviews.
7. Hypothetical answers describing what you would do in a future situation.
8. Showing related work experience. (Higher rank if successful during that experience.)
9. Opinion: self-descriptive statements trying to convince the interviewer how   great you are.
10. Answering with a lot of words but avoiding the actual question that was asked.

11. Awkward silence.

12. Lying.

Although companies do not have a formal hierarchy list, interviewers often rank candidates' answers based on a hierarchy of impressiveness. For example, if you are interviewing for a job in the commercial industry, your strongest answers should demonstrate how you made or saved money for your previous employers. While it's important to convey your strongest highlights, avoid memorizing verbatim answers.

To make a strong impression on the interviewer, focus on highlighting your accomplishments and results in previous roles. Be prepared to provide specific examples of how you contributed to the success of your previous employers, especially in areas that are relevant to the job you are interviewing for. By showcasing your ability to make a positive impact on the company's bottom line, you can demonstrate your value as a potential employee.

How we assess candidate potential.

Employers seek candidates who have the potential to grow and improve while performing well in their current role. During the interview process, interviewers evaluate certain traits to assess a candidate's potential for growth and development. I have used the following list as my guidance in the past to determine candidate potential:

- **Motivation**

High-potential candidates possess a strong drive to excel and achieve significant accomplishments, but their goals extend beyond their individual success. They also strive for collective objectives and demonstrate humility, investing time and effort to improve their skills and abilities in all areas. This dedication to both personal and collective growth sets them apart as exceptional candidates.

- **Curiosity**

Candidates who possess a desire for personal growth tend to have a natural inclination towards exploring new experiences, seeking knowledge, and receiving honest feedback. These individuals remain open to learning and embracing change, recognizing that personal development is a continual process that requires dedication and an eagerness to expand their horizons.

- **Insight**

The capacity to gather and interpret data in a way that reveals fresh perspectives and opportunities is a valuable trait that sets candidates apart. Being able to discern patterns and connect seemingly unrelated information helps in identifying new possibilities and finding innovative solutions. This ability to gather and make sense of information is a critical skill for success in many industries.

- **Engagement**

Being able to communicate a compelling vision effectively is a highly sought-after skill by employers. Those who possess a talent for using both emotion and logic to persuade others are especially valuable. The ability to connect with people on an emotional level, while also using logic to present a clear and persuasive message, is essential for successful communication. This skill can help build strong relationships, motivate teams, and drive the achievement of shared goals.

- **Determination**

The perseverance to pursue challenging objectives in the face of obstacles and the resilience to recover from setbacks. Hiring determined candidates can bring a sense of motivation and drive to the workplace, which can inspire others to work harder and achieve more. Determination is often an indicator of a candidate's passion for their work and their commitment to producing high-quality results. This quality can also help employers identify individuals who are likely to persevere through challenges and contribute to the company's success.

Understanding the perceptions that interviewers likely have.

Interviewers may ask questions based on your resume or as a follow-up to one of your answers. Understanding how others perceive your background is key to highlighting your strengths and mitigating shortcomings. For instance, having a strong track record with a well-respected company is an advantage.

Startups often prefer candidates with experience in both established and small companies. Large organizations are known for providing comprehensive training, which can be beneficial for a candidate's next job. However, startups have a different culture, and hiring managers may prefer candidates who have previous experience in an entrepreneurial environment to ensure that they understand the culture and are a good fit.

Academic credentials from renowned institutions, such as Harvard or Stanford, can be beneficial, but they do not guarantee success. Candidates who project arrogance due to their education may not make a good impression. It is important to be self-aware and demonstrate eagerness and capability to learn.

Candidates with a history of short-term employment may be viewed with suspicion, as it may suggest issues with skills or personality. During the interview process, it is crucial to uncover any history of inferior performance or conflict with management/co-workers.

Getting some extra help – Understanding the recruiters.

When you are going through an interview process, you might work with a recruiter, either an inside/corporate recruiter or an outside/third-party recruiter, commonly referred to as a "Headhunter" for executive-level roles. Regardless of the type of recruiter you work with, there are some basic commonalities to their job, the most important being that if you impress them, they often become your advocate.

Corporate Talent Acquisition Recruiters are given goals for the number of hires they need to fill at their company, with their job performance evaluated by the metric of "Time-to-Fill". Quality-of-Hire is also tracked in many companies, including retention, performance, and promotion of employees hired by that recruiter. If you can impress the recruiter, they can become an advocate to get you hired, as it reflects well on their job performance.

Outside recruiters, including headhunters, have a direct financial incentive to become advocates for strong candidates. Most are paid on a contingency basis, meaning they only receive payment if they fill the position. If you impress an outside recruiter, they will become an advocate for you, potentially introducing you to opportunities at multiple companies.

Understanding the incentives of recruiters will help you take advantage of their assistance, and building long-term professional relationships with good recruiters can benefit your career. However, it's important to be mindful of your actions, as behaving inappropriately can damage relationships. For example, directly contacting a hiring manager without informing your recruiter can lead to negative consequences and harm your chances of future opportunities.

How to Answer Behavioral-Based Interview Questions

Behavioral-based interview questions are based on the premise that past behavior is the best predictor of future behavior in similar situations. These questions are also known as competency-based, behavioral, situational-based, or performance-based interviews. There is a related style of questioning called skill-based interview questions. To succeed in these types of interviews, it's important to prepare in advance.

Situational-based interview questions are hypothetical, but the strongest answers are those that draw from actual experiences in comparable situations. To increase your chances of success, there is a simple exercise you can do before the interview. But before we get into that, let's cover some common advice for answering these types of questions.

Behavioral interviews are designed to test your ability to work well in various scenarios, including high-pressure situations, tight deadlines, and urgent needs. The interviewer wants to see if your decisions and attitude align with the qualities they're seeking in a candidate. You'll likely be asked to provide specific examples of times when you've been in similar situations.

To answer behavioral questions effectively, take some time to reflect on your past experiences and think about which ones are most relevant to each question. This will help you stay organized and confident during the interview. When answering, be sure to give a specific example and focus on the relevant details. Avoid providing unnecessary information that may distract from your main points.

One candidate I worked with was a borderline fit for the job on paper, but her well-prepared answers to my behavioral questions set her apart from all the other candidates. Her responses were exactly what we were looking for and she delivered them with confidence and detail. Even though the hiring manager wasn't impressed by her resume, she sailed through the rest of the process and got the job. If you want to interview successfully, follow her lead, and prepare strong examples that demonstrate the qualities the interviewer is seeking.

What is the standard advice on how to respond to behavioral-based interview questions?

Here is a list of what you can do to prepare for behavioral interview questions:

1. Examples should be tailored to the ideal profile.

2. Make a list of your previous efforts and significant achievements.

3. Formulate your answers using the STAR technique, which I will explain in this chapter.

4. Be succinct and precise in your answers.

Examples should be tailored to the ideal profile.

During a behavioral interview, it's important to remember that the interviewer is looking for specific qualities in a candidate. Your answers should provide clues that you are a good fit for the profile they're seeking. To tailor your responses to their needs, pay attention to the job description. For instance, if the position requires three years of experience and proficiency in certain software programs, you should be prepared to talk about situations where you used those programs or similar ones. By doing so, you'll show the interviewer that you have the skills they're looking for and increase your chances of landing the job.

Make a list of your previous efforts and significant achievements.

To succeed in a behavioral interview, it's crucial to spend time preparing in advance. Make a list of projects from your career that are relevant to the job you're applying for, and if you're early in your professional life, don't hesitate to use examples from your academic career if they're applicable. During the interview, be sure to include details of your experiences that demonstrate your qualifications for the job. In particular, explain how your actions led to success for your employer. If, for example, you were responsible for a significant increase in sales, be prepared to discuss the steps you took to achieve that outcome and how you can replicate that success in the future. By organizing your experiences and highlighting your achievements, you'll be well-equipped to impress the interviewer and secure the job.

Formulate your answers using the STAR technique.

The STAR technique (situation, task, action, and result) is the most popular method for answering behavioral interview questions in a clear and thorough way. Some people may refer to it as SOAR (situation, obstacle, action, and result), but it's essentially the same thing. By using this technique, you can break down your responses into easy-to-follow components that effectively convey your experience in a previous job. Each element of STAR offers a framework for telling your story when answering behavioral-based interview questions. With this technique, you'll be well-prepared to respond to questions in a way that showcases your skills and achievements and increases your chances of landing the job. Here is an explanation of each stage and an example:

- **Situation**

Describe a situation relevant to the question asked that you have faced in your work, and any essential facts the interviewer should be aware of. Prioritize pertinent information that relates to the position you are looking for.

Consider the following scenario: *"Our team had a backlog of articles that needed to be submitted and authorized by the customer in my previous job as an internal copywriter. The editors imposed strict deadlines on us in order for us to finish the items in our queue, which caused me stress."*

- **Task**

Tell the interviewer about the responsibilities that you had in this scenario. This explains the specifics of what you needed to accomplish on behalf of your former company to reach a goal. As I will explain later in the chapter, this is the least important part of the STAR technique.

"My job was to make sure that over the following five days, I produced and submitted three articles to fulfill the fifteen-article goal set by my project manager to assist the team in catching up."

- **Action**

Explain the steps that you took to meet your deadline and accomplish the objective you set for yourself. Create a list of the top talents that you want to communicate to the interviewer for this stage, which should emphasize the skill you are attempting to convey to the interviewer.

"Over the course of this period, I set up three two-hour time slots in my schedule to work on these three articles. If I had any concerns, I called the project manager, and I shut out any other distractions by listening to classical music to maintain my concentration on writing."

- **Result**

Define the results achieved due to your activities. When feasible, provide statistics or specific quantifiable outcomes and how they impacted the business at the time. You want to give a clear timeline, completion timeline, and the impact of your decisions.

"I ended up producing and submitting eight articles at the end of the week, more than double my planned goal. As a result, we were able to meet our deadline and ended up expanding our relationships with those clients."

Be succinct and precise in your answers.

When answering behavioral interview questions, it's important to keep your responses concise, ideally under two minutes. To achieve this, consider practicing with a mentor or friend who can help you focus on the main points while keeping your answers brief. Alternatively, record yourself answering the questions and listen back to assess the length and quality of your answers. Keep in mind that the interviewer may shift gears and ask different questions, so be prepared to adapt accordingly. By preparing in advance and delivering concise, relevant responses, you'll make a strong impression and increase your chances of landing the job.

Examples of Behavioral-based interview questions:

1. Describe the most challenging situation you have had to deal with in the last year.

2. Describe a moment when you exceeded your manager's expectations to help a customer.

3. Tell us about a time when a colleague needed motivation and what you did to help them.

4. Tell us about a time when your workload was a problem. What steps did you take to address this problem?

5. Have you ever felt pressured to meet a deadline? What methods did you use to deal with this problem?

6. Describe a time when you committed a blunder that had a negative impact on your team. How did you deal with that situation?

7. Tell me about a time that you had to rapidly pick up a new skill. What was the outcome, and how did you go about learning your new skill?

8. Tell me about when you had to pitch an idea to upper management. What was the outcome?

9. Have you ever had a disagreement with a coworker about the project's direction? What did you do to come to a compromise with your coworker?

Using the STAR method, here is an example of a successful behavioral-based interview answer:

Describe the most challenging situation you have had to deal with in the past year.

"I received a call from a client a year ago regarding a complaint he had about the software we provided. He stated that he wanted to cancel his account with us because the software had shut down while he was working on a critical project for his company. I asked him to take me through what had happened step by step so that I could better understand what had happened."

"After hearing his story, I decided that we should offer to refund the money he had paid for the month that the problem occurred. I called my manager and explained the situation to get her approval. Then I worked with one of our engineers to figure out the technical problem the client

had with our software. I was able to refund him the money and fix the issues with his software at no additional charge. This action resulted in retaining the account, and the consistent payments from a top client, contributing to a profit increase for my company."

This answer is successful because it takes the interviewer through a success story where you are the star of that story, and your company benefited by having you as their employee. It mostly follows the STAR method but illustrates why I am telling you that there is a more effective, and efficient method to prepare for a behavioral-based interview.

The best way to prepare to successfully answer behavioral-based interview questions.

1. Start with one or more blank sheets of paper and turn them horizontally to be in a landscape layout. (Of course, you can do this digitally if you prefer.)
2. Draw two vertical lines down the page so that you create three equal columns.
3. At the top of the left column write "Situation", center column "Action", and on the right "Results".

4. Re-read the ideal profile you wrote or the job advertisement, the duties, requirements, and any other parts that describe what the company is looking for in the person that they hire.

5. Using only bullet points, start listing specific examples from your career that relate to the ideal profile.

6. After you have put as many relevant examples as you can recall, set this page aside and when you remember another fitting example, come back to it and jot it down. (This might take a couple of days.)

7. Once you have all the most relevant examples, re-write your page and rank them so that your best examples are listed at the top (the ones that you don't want to leave the interview without making sure you mention them.), and then list the remainder in descending order of impressiveness.

To improve your performance in behavioral-based interviews, consider using the SAR (Situation, Action, Results) technique instead of STAR (Situation, Task, Action, Results). While tasks and responsibilities are important, they're typically less significant than the situation, action, and results of your story. Focusing on these elements will make it easier to remember a greater number of examples and their details. When answering questions, start with the situation, describe the action you took, and conclude with the results you achieved. By keeping it simple and straightforward, you'll be more productive and confident.

Preparing with the SAR exercise before your interview can help you recall examples and deliver a confident, successful answer. Taking a moment to recall your list of examples, choosing the best one for the question, and sharing your success story demonstrates confidence and impresses the interviewer. Without this preparation, candidates may struggle to recall examples from their past, leading to a less confident and less impressive performance. To access this exercise and other helpful resources, check out the **COMPANION WORKBOOK: The Ultimate Guide to Successful Job Interviewing**.

Final behavioral-based interview insights.

Many candidates dislike behavioral-based interview questions because they believe they can make up stories to get hired. However, these types of questions are just one tool used to make hiring decisions. Experienced recruiters and hiring managers can spot inconsistencies and check on claims made in answers.

Candidates who are dishonest may save the interviewer time by demonstrating why they should not be hired.

The most common mistake candidates make when answering behavioral-based interview questions is to avoid answering them altogether. For example, if a candidate is asked for an example and responds with a vague non-answer like "I deal with that all the time..." or "I have many clients who do that...", they have failed to provide a specific example related to the question. After a few vague answers, most interviewers will eliminate the candidate from consideration.

Another mistake is not listening to the entire question. Candidates often focus on the example they want to use and stop listening to the interviewer. However, there may be multiple parts to the question, and candidates need to listen carefully to provide an appropriate answer.

To prepare for behavioral-based interview questions, write out bullet points for success stories and practice saying them aloud. Avoid memorizing verbatim answers and speak naturally during the interview. Remember that interview questions are chosen to determine if a candidate fits the ideal profile for the job. Answers should include examples of skills, temperament, experience, and talent that match what the company is looking for.

Canned, disingenuous answers are not recommended. Instead, memorize bullet points and speak naturally during the interview. Interviewers are also assessing personality fit, and coming across as fake or reciting answers can be detrimental to a candidate's success.

Quick reference summary:

1. Prepare ahead of time using the SAR exercise.
2. Do not make up examples.
3. Give real examples from your experience.
4. Listen to the entire question.
5. Practice saying your examples aloud before the interview.
6. Relate all your examples to the ideal profile.
7. Focus on the main points that you need to make.

How to Answer the Most Common Tough Interview Questions

Many job applicants have experienced the sinking feeling of being caught off-guard by unexpected or tough interview questions. While it's impossible to anticipate exactly what interviewers will ask, being familiar with common difficult questions, their purpose, and how to approach them can help job seekers feel more confident and ready.

Interview questions are designed to assess how well a candidate matches the ideal profile that an organization is looking for. For example, the classic "tell me about yourself" question has stumped many candidates. I have seen two types of candidates fail this question: the overconfident and the intimidated. Later in this chapter, I will provide tips on how to avoid these pitfalls.

Successful candidates typically prepare for tough interview questions in advance, taking the time to tailor answers to a specific organization or employer. This can make interviews go more smoothly and make applicants more impressive to interviewers. Some tough questions push candidates to think critically and creatively, while others catch candidates off guard.

No matter how challenging an interview may seem, getting hired depends on how prepared a candidate is relative to other applicants. The key is to demonstrate how well you match the job requirements and specifications. Your answers should be concise and relevant, connecting your experiences to the ideal profile.

Understanding the job and candidate profile can provide insights into the questions you may be asked during an interview. Successful interview preparation often involves practicing answering questions with a partner, recording and listening to your answers, and practicing until you are comfortable and confident. Avoid memorizing answers verbatim and instead focus on the main points you want to make and speak naturally.

Despite being a great fit on paper, I have interviewed thousands of job candidates who fell short in the interview. On the other hand, candidates who seemed less qualified on paper impressed me in the interview. To help you succeed, take a closer look at some of the most common difficult interview questions, and examples of how to answer them.

Interview questions that are difficult to answer and how to respond to them.

"Tell me about yourself."

Reason we ask: The interviewer is trying to evaluate how much of a match you are to what they want to hire. This question/statement is a quick way for us to gather certain information; do you understand the job and what we are looking for? Do you have the education and/or experience we want? For some jobs, we are evaluating your presentation skills.

Answering the open-ended question "Tell me about yourself" is an excellent chance to showcase how you align with what the interviewer is seeking. Many candidates make the mistake of giving long-winded, irrelevant answers that lack detail related to the job. For this reason, it is helpful to take a chronological approach, starting from when you began your career or education up to your current position. Your answer should be concise and no longer than 30-60 seconds, and it should include relevant achievements that demonstrate how you align with the job requirements.

When responding, you should address both the skills and personality traits required for the position. Avoid generic responses like "Unique" or "Hardworking" and instead, connect your experience, skills, and personality traits to what the employer is looking for in the ideal candidate.

Highlight specific areas where your background matches the job requirements, such as your education, experience with specific software programs or languages, or other skills that are relevant to the position. If you can, try to connect a personal trait to the company culture or the job description.

To make your answer stand out, add a brief statement that sets you apart from other candidates. Specifically, you should include your Unique Value Proposition (UVP). Your UVP should be a brief statement that clearly explains your skills, experience, and unique strengths in a way that appeals to this employer. Based on your research or knowledge about the company or industry, mention something about yourself that makes you more qualified for the job than most other candidates. To learn more about the UVP, please read my book *SoaringME **The Ultimate Guide to Successful Job Searching***.

Matching your skills and personality to the ideal profile is critical in creating a strong response to this question and developing compelling positioning and closing statements. Spend time crafting a concise and powerful answer that demonstrates your ability to meet the job requirements.

What to avoid: Throughout my years of conducting interviews, I have noticed two types of candidates who consistently fail when it comes to answering the questions, "Tell me about yourself", or "Why are you a good fit for this position?" The first type is the overconfident candidate who tends to use clichés and self-promoting language without providing any evidence to back up their claims. I once had a candidate repeatedly describe themselves as an "All-star" several times during an interview without offering any examples that supported this statement. Needless to say, he did not come across as convincing and did not move forward in the interview process.

The second type of candidate who often struggles with this question is the intimidated candidate. They may not see how their skills and experiences align with the position and fail to mention them in their answer. However, it is crucial to research the job and company beforehand and identify the ways in which you are a good match. Your answer should not be about bragging but about demonstrating your qualifications for the position.

Confidence is key when answering this question. Be sure to highlight your relevant experiences and skills that make you a strong fit for the position. Avoid using generic language and provide concrete examples to support your claims. Remember, it is not just about showcasing your skills and experiences, but also about demonstrating how they align with the job requirements and company culture. By preparing and delivering a strong answer, you can stand out as a top candidate for the job.

"What are your biggest weaknesses?"

Reason we ask: Your answer to this question should tell us how self-aware you are, and if you have a weakness that makes you not compatible with the job or company.

When asked about your biggest weakness, it's important to understand that the interviewer may also phrase the question as "What is something your boss has told you that you need to work on?" or "What is one thing that you would change about yourself?" The key to answering this question is sincerity. Avoid presenting a positive trait as a flaw or mentioning a personality trait, as these responses can come across as insincere. Instead, discuss an actual professional shortcoming that you have identified, worked on, improved upon, and that will not negatively impact your performance in the job you are interviewing for. This demonstrates self-awareness and a commitment to professional growth.

Example answer of a candidate interviewing for an Executive Assistant role: *"In my previous job as a Copywriter, I lacked enough creativity to consistently produce new original content. I took workshops and I got better, but I never felt like it was what I was best at. I'm good at writing and staying organized, so I decided to find a career that was a better match for my strengths."*

The creativity needed to be a Copywriter is not required to be an exceptionally good Executive Assistant. The answer displays self-awareness and the ability to improve but does not make the interviewer doubt that the candidate is a match for the role.

What to avoid: It is crucial to avoid certain responses when asked about your biggest weakness in a job interview. The worst answer would be to claim that you do not have any weaknesses. This response portrays a lack of self-awareness and raises a red flag that you might be a difficult employee. The second-worst answer is to mention a skill from the ideal profile for the job, which could be perceived as a lack of preparation and effort. Cliché responses like "I'm a workaholic" or "I can be too driven by my work" come across as insincere and should be avoided. It's important to choose an actual professional weakness that you have identified, fixed or improved, and are continuing to work on.

"Why should I hire you over somebody else?"

Reason we ask: This answer will tell the interviewer how well you understand the job, how much of a match you are to what we want to hire, and some insight into your enthusiasm.

To prepare for "Why should I hire you over somebody else?" question, focus on practicing for "Tell me about yourself" and

"What is your greatest strength?" questions. A successful answer should demonstrate your understanding of the job and the ideal candidate profile. Provide a concise overview of how your experience and skills align with the position. Show why you are the best candidate for the job and the company without comparing yourself to others. Create a compelling and succinct explanation of why your services are valuable to the business.

Example answer for a candidate interviewing for a Data Engineer role: *"I believe that my experience lines up well with what you are looking for. My experience is directly transferable, and I have strong coding skills in both Python and R. More than just being a technical fit, I am passionate about what you're doing here and would really enjoy working on the types of projects you need done."*

What to avoid: Many candidates give a rehearsed answer to this question, which can sound artificial and insincere. It's best to avoid discussing other candidates or being negative about them, as it may indicate that you have difficulties working with others.

"Why are you interested in this job?"

Reason we ask: The answer to this question gives the interviewer insights into your career goals; how much you know about this position and company, whether you did your research, what your motivation is, how strong your motivation is, what is most important to you. All of those help us determine how much of a fit you are. Applicants who simply want any job become employees that do not stay long, and this question is an attempt to screen them out of the process.

Your response to this question should showcase that you have taken the time to research the company and the position, and that you are enthusiastic about the opportunity. While it is important to connect your background to the ideal profile, the focus of your answer should be on the company itself. Identify two or three unique attributes of the company's culture, history, products, or reputation that differentiate it from other employers. Your response should demonstrate that you are motivated, professional, and have a genuine interest in the company and the position.

Example answer:

"I'm extremely impressed with this PQRS Therapeutics reputation, and I think that your science might be the next big breakthrough. My PhD was focused on immunology, and for the past five years I have been working with Immuno-Oncology cell therapies. I think you are on the

right path with what you're developing, and I would love to be a part of advancing this type of science."

What to avoid: Mentioning compensation or benefits and displaying a lack of enthusiasm in your tone or body language are two mistakes to avoid when answering this question. Focusing too much on salary and perks can give the impression that you are not passionate about the job or the company, but only interested in what you can get out of it. Similarly, a disinterested tone or negative body language can give the impression that you are not fully invested in the opportunity, which can be a turn-off for the interviewer.

"What is your biggest achievement?"

Reason we ask: The answer to this question should give the interviewer insight into both your skills and your personality. When you choose what you consider to be your biggest achievement, it gives us insight into what you consider to be most important. Understanding what your priorities are in the workplace will help us determine if you are a good fit for our company culture. We also need a certain level of skill in the people that we hire, so understanding what you did and how well you did it for your biggest achievement will inform us about your skill-level.

Many people struggle with answering this question because they are not used to promoting themselves. However, it is a vital opportunity to showcase your accomplishments and how they align with the job you are interviewing for. Your answer should not only demonstrate an achievement but also how it could positively impact the company or team, whether it is through boosting sales or improving collaboration. Depending on the job requirements, you may also highlight your personal achievements if they show that you are a good fit. Practicing your answer beforehand can help you feel more at ease with selling yourself during the interview.

Example: The startup software company is hiring an outside sales representative. A competitive nature is a must have trait. They would prefer previous experience, but it is not required.

Answer 1: *"When I began in my current position the company had not even launched its first software program. It was a challenging start, but I built relationships with key decision makers within our target market* *and ended up winning sales representative of the year out of our team of twenty."*

Answer 2: *"I am highly driven and results-oriented, but since this will be my first professional job after graduating, I'd have to say that my greatest achievement to-date has been that I was named captain of my college soccer team three years in a row. I love what I know about your software, and I look forward to being a top performer for you, like I was in my athletic career."*

What to avoid: Do not give a vague response and instead, use a specific achievement. It's essential to be honest and avoid taking undue credit for something that was not solely your accomplishment. If you were part of a team, make sure to explain your significant contribution to the success. This answer should be backed by specific examples and not be merely a general statement. Be prepared for follow-up questions that may scrutinize your individual role in the achievement.

"What would your co-workers say about you?"

Reason we ask: Being self-aware is a particularly important soft skill for most organizations. Understanding how your behavior is perceived by others allows you to get along better with co-workers and to be more productive. Your answer to this question should give us an idea of how self-aware you are, and about your personality. We will compare your answer to all other evidence we have or observe about you. We want to see if you would be a good fit for the company culture and this question helps us make that determination.

Before the interview, take time to evaluate your own strengths and skills, and then compare them to the ideal profile that the company is seeking. Make a list of anecdotes from your work that showcase these skills. When answering this question, highlight one or at most two of your strengths that align with the job requirements. Start by telling the interviewer about these strengths and then back them up with examples from your experience.

Example answer: *"In my current role as a data engineer, most of my co-workers would describe me as a creative problem-solver. Just last quarter my team and I encountered an integration problem that we couldn't find an existing solution for. After analyzing a couple of work-around options, I presented my ideas to the team, and we worked together to solve the issues."*

This answer demonstrates both that the candidate is a creative problem-solver, but also that he/she works well within a team.

What to avoid: It's crucial to be honest while answering the interview questions. You should never fabricate skills or give false examples. The interviewers may cross-check some of your responses with others who have interviewed you. Making up skills or experiences that you do not possess is not only unprofessional but also a surefire way to lose the opportunity. **Being dishonest is the fastest and most sure-fire way to guarantee that you don't get the job.**

"What are your biggest strengths?"

Reason why we ask: This is a straightforward way for us to assess what you are best at and if that matches what we wish to hire. Your answer may also give us further insight into your personality, such as determining if you are self-aware and our view of a good fit.

The employer schedules an interview with you because they are interested in learning more about the qualities that you possess. Always keep in mind that there are other applicants competing with you for the job. It is advantageous to highlight a skill that sets you apart from other applicants, or that you excel in.

Notable strengths do not necessarily have to be hard skills; some employers are looking for the right personality that can be trained. Therefore, behavioral qualities such as tenacity or resilience might be essential when analyzing the ideal profile for the job.

When describing your greatest strength, it is important to provide evidence that supports your claim. You should give an example of a time when you displayed this strength and how it produced a positive result. A strong example that demonstrates your skill is crucial to make your answer stand out from other candidates. Lastly, your answer should tie back to the job you are interviewing for. You can simply add a brief statement at the end of your answer that explains how this strength will contribute to your success in the position.

Follow these steps to prepare for this question:

1. Make a list of your biggest strengths, experience, education, training, hard and soft skills.
2. Self-assess and rank the skills on your list or the order in which they are your strongest attributes.

3. Make a list of the desired qualities based on your understanding of the ideal profile.
4. Start with the first listed attribute that the company desires, and if it is listed as one of your top strengths, this should be the focus of your answer. If not, go to the second listed attribute on the company list. Continue until you find a genuine strength of yours that is highest on both lists.

If you can't find an overlap between the job requirements and your strengths, but you believe that one of your strengths will be valuable in this position, you must tailor your response to emphasize how this skill is relevant to the job. It's okay if you have two strengths to highlight, but keep your answer brief, lasting no more than two minutes.

Example answer: *"I have excellent organizational skills. While I was going to college full-time, I also worked twenty hours a week in the accounting department at XYZ Corp. At that job my primary responsibility was consolidation of overseas quarterly financial reports, and my boss never had to make an adjustment to any of my work. I was able to complete my accounting degree on time and graduated with honors. I know my ability to organize my time and complete projects accurately will help me be successful in this role."*

The impression this answer gives is that not only is this candidate organized, but also smart, hard-working, and motivated.

What to avoid: The way you answer this question can reveal a lot about your character and suitability for the job. Overconfidence may suggest that you are not open to constructive criticism and unwilling to improve. Conversely, being too modest may lead the interviewer to question your self-assurance and ability to excel in the role. The key is to strike a balance between confidence and humility, demonstrating that you are self-aware and coachable. Choose a strength that is specific and relevant to the job, avoiding generic or overly common answers.

"Why are you leaving your current job?" / "Why did you leave your previous job?"

Reason we ask: This question does inform us about your motivation, and whether this career move makes enough sense to lead us to believe that you will be a long-term employee for us. But the tricky part of this question is how much we can learn about your personality.

Complaining about your current or previous job, colleagues, or bosses during an interview can leave a negative impression on potential employers, even if your complaints are genuine. Instead, focus on what you want to achieve in your next career step and match those desires with what the new job offers. Always try to relate your answer back to how you are a good fit for the opportunity. The approach to answering this question might differ depending on how you left your previous employment. Therefore, I am providing some scenarios and example answers to guide you.

Example answer for someone who voluntarily left/are leaving on good terms with their employer:

"I am grateful for the opportunity that I had at ABC Company, it was a wonderful experience but it's just time for me to take on a new challenge and show that I can accomplish even more than I already have. Your company will provide me with the opportunity to do that."

Example answer for someone who voluntarily left/are leaving on less than good terms with their employer:

"I learned a lot in my time with ABC Company, but over time I realized what I really need is an opportunity that is going to both challenge me and allow me to work with a product that I can be passionate about. I really like what I've learned about your company and products. This is a better fit for me and where I want to take my career."

Example answers for someone who was laid-off by their employer not due to performance:

"Unfortunately, my company went through a re-structuring in April. Since I was one of the most recent hires, I was part of a group that was let go. I have received an above average performance review, and my manager will be one of my references. The work that I had done well in that position is very similar to your position so I'm confident I will get up to speed very quickly."

Example answer for someone who was terminated by their employer:

"When I was originally hired it was because they were looking to bring a different skill set into ABC Company. I made appropriate changes and we did increase sales by 33%, but it quickly became clear that the President and I have different styles. I learned that to thrive, I need an innovative and collaborative environment, which is exactly what I see that your company promotes itself to be."

Notice that this answer is not negative towards the previous employer or boss, makes the point that at least some of the work done was good, and brings it all back to being a good fit for this new job. It does not give every detail about being fired and does not tell a lie. You should expect follow-up questions about some of the details, but continue to be concise, honest, positive, and professional. If you made a mistake at your previous job, explain how you have learned from it and why it will not be a problem for your next employer.

What to avoid: It is not appropriate to share negative experiences or personal conflicts with previous employers during an interview. Over-explaining or becoming emotional about your reasons for leaving a previous job should be avoided as well. Honesty is important, but it is never acceptable to lie about how you left a previous job. Remember that background checks are typically conducted, and if dishonesty is discovered, it could lead to termination from the new job.

"What are your salary expectations?"
(See the later chapter entitled *The Job Offer.*)

Successfully Answer Technical Interview Questions

Technical interviews are designed to evaluate a candidate's skill level in a specific area that is essential for success in a technical job. This type of interview is commonly used in industries such as tech, engineering, and finance/accounting. The questions asked will vary depending on the specific technology or skill being evaluated and can differ from one interviewer to the next. In this chapter, I provide an overview of what to expect in a technical interview.

To prepare for a technical interview, there are several online resources available that provide up-to-date questions that are being asked at specific companies. While the questions asked may vary from one interviewer to the next, preparing for commonly asked questions can help you feel more confident and increase your chances of success. It is also recommended that you not only research technical interview questions at the company you are applying to, but also their competitors, to prepare more thoroughly.

It is important to note that technical interviews are designed to screen for skills, and it is crucial that you have a solid understanding of the specific technology or skill being evaluated. By doing your research and practicing your skills, you can approach a technical interview with confidence and increase your chances of landing the job.

You can expect technical interview questions to cover these areas.

1. Your experience. (Including behavioral-based questions focused on the technical aspects of the job.)
2. Brainteaser questions to test your applied thinking.
3. White boarding. While the actual whiteboard has been going out of style as of late, there will be some variation in coding interviews to evaluate your current skills.

During a technical interview, it is not just your technical skills that are evaluated. The interviewer is also looking to assess your personality and soft skills. If you are being considered for a team-oriented position, communication is a critical skill that the interviewer will be evaluating. Solving a problem is one thing, but being able to communicate your thought process and ideas is equally important. A successful employee is someone who can work collaboratively with others to achieve a common goal. Thus, candidates who engage in a back-and-forth conversation with the interviewer while discussing their problem-solving process tend to be more successful in interviews.

Also, intellectual curiosity and passion for technology are far too overlooked in technical interviews. **Companies are much more likely to hire a person with passion who can be coached-up on their hard skills, than an expert who lacks enthusiasm for their work.**

Questions about experience can be direct questions about what you have worked on, or like the questions I covered in the chapter on *How to answer behavioral-based interview questions.*

Examples of technical interview behavioral-based questions.

"Tell me about a project you worked on that failed."

And *"Tell me about the most challenging tech problem you have faced in the past couple of years. How did you solve it?"*

What are we looking for? You have the ability to overcome challenges and work well within a team.

"Tell me about a tech project that you have worked on in your spare time."

What are we looking for? Your passion.

"Tell me about a time where you were asked to do something that you had never done before. How did you go about it?"

What are we looking for? Ability to work independently, and your self-motivation.

Examples of technical interview direct questions.

"What online resources do you use to help you do your job?"

What are we looking for? Your passion, resourcefulness, and ingenuity.

"How do you keep your technical skills current?"

What are we looking for? Your passion and professionalism.

"Pretend I'm not a tech person; how would you explain 'X' to me?"

('X' represents the technology used in this job or your past job.)

What are we looking for? Your communication skills, especially if the job will require you to explain things to less technical people. And, to a lesser extent, gives some insight into your technical knowledge.

Technical interviews are renowned for their unorthodox and abstract questions. The purpose of such interview questions is to assess your thought process and how well you can reason your way through a problem. The emphasis is not on providing the correct answer to an insignificant question. We are looking for individuals who can think quickly and support their responses with a sound explanation. Thus, it is crucial to communicate your logic effectively during the interview process. While solving a problem, it is best to articulate your thought process in real-time. Even if you take a wrong turn, it is acceptable to explain how you recognized your error and found a better approach.

Examples of these curveball questions:

"How many golf balls would it take to fill an SUV?"

"A scientist puts a bacterium in a Petri dish at noon. Every minute, the bacteria divide into two. At exactly 1 p.m. the Petri dish is full. At what time was the dish half full?"

"Describe the internet to someone who woke up from a 30-year coma."

As I recommended earlier, do your research on what companies in your industry are currently using.

Many companies use challenging scenarios or problems to evaluate your expertise in the job role. These questions are designed to test your problem-solving abilities and how well you can apply your knowledge and skills to real-world situations. It is important to remain calm and focused during these technical interviews and answer the questions to the best of your abilities. Don't be afraid to ask for clarification or additional information if needed. Remember, the interviewer is not necessarily looking for the correct answer but wants to see how you approach the problem and your ability to think critically and creatively.

Here are suggestions to prepare for this part of the technical interview:

1. Study for technical interviews through current books, websites, and online videos to learn the latest questions you are likely to be asked.

2. Study the technology used at the company and the position.

3. Focus on refreshing the basic knowledge for that technology.

If you are unsure about the technology or the question, it is best to clarify and admit that you do not have the answer but try to demonstrate your knowledge of related technologies. Technical interviews are not just about getting the right answer but also about showcasing your thought process and problem-solving skills. To prepare for these interviews, it is important to have a strong foundation in relevant areas and demonstrate your ability to approach a problem from a high-level perspective. Avoid getting sidetracked by minor details and stay focused on the main issue at hand.

Common Corporate Finance Interview Questions

During my interviews with candidates for corporate finance roles, I usually kick things off with an open-ended question like, "Tell me about yourself" or "Give me an overview of your background." However, I've noticed a common theme among the worst responses: candidates tend to talk about the businesses they worked for rather than their own role in those companies. While it's helpful to understand the context of the companies where you've worked, when I ask these questions, I'm really interested in what you did while you were there.

As a finance candidate, it's crucial to demonstrate how your previous work experience aligns with the requirements of the role you're interviewing for. Understanding the company's operations is important, but talking about the company to the exclusion of your own accomplishments and responsibilities can detract from your candidacy. In addition to the "Tell me about yourself" question, there are other common interview questions that finance candidates should be prepared to answer.

Interview questions for earlier career corporate finance roles.

"What experience do you have with financial modeling?"

Reason we ask: Your answer to this question should provide us with an understanding of your expertise in financial modeling and your ability to create, analyze, and interpret complex financial models. We want to assess your proficiency in using various financial modeling techniques, tools, and software, as well as your ability to effectively communicate the insights gained from these models to inform decision-making.

When asked about your experience with financial modeling, it's important to discuss specific projects or tasks you have undertaken in previous roles. The interviewer may also phrase the question as "Can you provide an example of a financial model you have built?" or "How have you used financial modeling to support strategic decisions?" Highlight the types of financial models you have created, the tools you used, and the impact your work had on the organization.

Example answer: "In my previous role as a Financial Analyst, I was responsible for creating and maintaining various financial models to support our team's decision-making process. This included building discounted cash flow models, three-statement models, and scenario analyses for our company's capital investments and potential M&A activities. I used Excel and other financial modeling software to create these models and worked closely with different departments to gather the necessary data. My models helped inform our strategic decisions and ultimately contributed to the company's growth and profitability."

This answer demonstrates the candidate's hands-on experience with financial modeling, their familiarity with different types of models, and their ability to collaborate with various stakeholders to drive informed decision-making.

What to avoid: When answering this question, avoid providing overly general or vague responses that do not showcase your expertise in financial modeling. Refrain from discussing unrelated experiences or skills, as this may be perceived as a lack of focus or preparation. Additionally, avoid downplaying the importance of financial modeling, as it is a critical skill for professionals in corporate finance roles.

"What are some of the most important financial reports you have prepared, and what was your role in their preparation?"

Reason we ask: This question is designed to assess your experience and knowledge of financial reporting and your ability to work with financial data. It provides insight into the type of financial reports you have prepared and your role in their preparation, giving the interviewer a better understanding of your skills and suitability for the entry-level corporate finance role.

When asked about the financial reports you have prepared and your role in their preparation, it's important to provide a clear and concise overview of your experience. The interviewer may also ask follow-up questions to delve deeper into your knowledge and experience.

Example answer: "During my previous internship, I was responsible for preparing financial reports such as income statements, balance sheets, and cash flow statements. My role involved collecting and analyzing data from various sources, reconciling accounts, and ensuring the accuracy and completeness of the reports.

I also assisted in the preparation of quarterly and annual financial statements and collaborated with cross-functional teams to ensure compliance with accounting standards and regulations. In addition, I gained experience in using financial software such as QuickBooks and Excel to process and analyze financial data."

This answer highlights the candidate's experience in preparing financial reports and their understanding of accounting standards and regulations.

What to avoid: When answering this question, avoid exaggerating or overstating your experience or responsibility in the preparation of financial reports. Also, avoid mentioning financial reports that are irrelevant or not related to the position you are applying for. It's important to provide specific and relevant examples of your experience and be prepared to answer follow-up questions.

"How would you value X company?"

Reason we ask: Your answer to this question should demonstrate your understanding of various valuation methods and their applicability in different situations. We want to assess your ability to select the most appropriate valuation technique for a given company and the rationale behind your choice. This will help us gauge your analytical skills and your capacity to effectively apply financial concepts in real-world scenarios.

When asked about valuing a specific company, it's important to discuss the different valuation methods you would consider and explain why you would choose a particular method for the given company. The interviewer may also phrase the question as "What factors would you consider when valuing a company?" or "Which valuation method do you think is most appropriate for X industry?" Be prepared to justify your choice and provide insights into your thought process.

Example answer: "To value Company X, I would first analyze the industry and the company's financial performance. Depending on the nature of the business, its growth prospects, and the availability of financial information, I would choose an appropriate valuation method. For instance, if Company X is a stable, mature company with a predictable cash flow, I would use the Discounted Cash Flow (DCF) method to estimate its intrinsic value. Alternatively, if Company X operates in a highly competitive industry with significant growth potential, I might consider using valuation multiples such as EV/EBITDA or P/E, comparing it to similar companies in the same sector. Ultimately, my choice of valuation method would depend on the specific circumstances and available information for Company X."

This answer demonstrates the candidate's understanding of different valuation methods and their ability to adapt their approach based on the company's characteristics and industry context.

What to avoid: When answering this question, avoid providing overly simplistic responses that do not showcase your knowledge of various valuation methods or your ability to apply them in practice. Refrain from focusing solely on one valuation method without considering other possibilities, as this may be perceived as a lack of flexibility or critical thinking. Additionally, avoid neglecting the importance of understanding the company's industry, financial performance, and growth prospects when determining the most appropriate valuation approach.

"Can you explain how you would go about forecasting revenue for a new product or business line, and what factors would you consider in your analysis?"

Reason we ask: This question is important to determine your ability to forecast revenue for a new product or business line, which is a crucial skill for entry-level corporate finance roles. Your answer should demonstrate your understanding of the key factors that impact revenue forecasting and your ability to use data analysis and modeling to make accurate predictions.

Example answer: "To forecast revenue for a new product or business line, I would start by analyzing the market demand for the product or service. I would conduct market research to identify the target audience, their needs, and their willingness to pay for the product. I would also consider the competitive landscape and the pricing strategies of the competitors.

Next, I would estimate the costs associated with producing and selling the product or service, including raw materials, labor, and marketing expenses. I would also factor in any fixed costs, such as rent or equipment, and variable costs, such as shipping or distribution costs.

Once I have a clear understanding of the market demand and costs, I would use financial modeling techniques to create a revenue forecast. I would adjust the model based on different scenarios, such as changes in pricing or market conditions, to identify potential risks and opportunities.

Overall, my approach to revenue forecasting involves a thorough analysis of market demand, costs, and financial modeling techniques to create an accurate forecast."

This answer demonstrates the candidate's ability to think critically and use data analysis to make informed decisions.

What to avoid: When answering this question, avoid giving vague or incomplete answers. Do not make assumptions about the market demand or the costs associated with the product or service. Instead, focus on providing a detailed overview of your approach to revenue forecasting, including the factors you consider and the techniques you use. Avoid making unrealistic or overly optimistic revenue projections without proper justification.

"Can you explain the differences between GAAP and IFRS accounting standards, and how they impact financial reporting?"

Reason we ask: This question assesses your knowledge of accounting standards and how they affect financial reporting. It shows your ability to work within regulatory frameworks and adapt to different accounting principles, which are crucial skills for an entry-level corporate finance role.

Example answer: "GAAP (Generally Accepted Accounting Principles) and IFRS (International Financial Reporting Standards) are two sets of accounting standards used in the United States and internationally, respectively. While both frameworks share some similarities, they have key differences in terms of their approach to revenue recognition, financial statement presentation, and accounting for certain financial instruments.

For example, GAAP typically requires companies to recognize revenue when it is earned, while IFRS allows for revenue recognition when it is probable that the economic benefits associated with the transaction will flow to the company. Additionally, GAAP requires the presentation of multiple financial statements, while IFRS consolidates some of these statements.

Understanding these differences is important because it can impact financial reporting, as companies that operate across borders may need to use both frameworks. It is also important to stay up to date with any changes to these frameworks, as they are subject to revision."

This answer demonstrates the candidate's understanding of the differences between GAAP and IFRS, and how these standards can affect financial reporting.

What to avoid: When answering this question, avoid providing a surface-level explanation that does not show a deep understanding of the accounting principles. Avoid oversimplifying or confusing GAAP and IFRS, as this may indicate a lack of familiarity with the accounting standards. Instead, provide specific examples of how these standards can impact financial reporting and demonstrate a clear understanding of the differences between the two frameworks.

"How do you assess the financial viability of a potential investment opportunity, and what factors do you consider in your analysis?"

Reason we ask: Your answer to this question will provide insight into your ability to evaluate the financial viability of investment opportunities and the factors you consider when conducting your analysis. This information will help us determine if you have the necessary skills and knowledge to succeed in an entry-level corporate finance role.

When asked about assessing the financial viability of an investment opportunity, it's essential to provide a clear and concise overview of your approach, highlighting the key principles, methods, and tools you employ. The interviewer may also phrase the question as "Can you discuss your investment analysis process and the key factors you consider?"

Example answer: "When assessing the financial viability of an investment opportunity, I first analyze the potential return on investment (ROI) and payback period. I also consider the risks involved, including market and industry risks, as well as any legal or regulatory risks. Other factors I evaluate include the company's financial history, competitive landscape, and growth potential.

To ensure a comprehensive analysis, I conduct a SWOT analysis (strengths, weaknesses, opportunities, and threats) and develop a detailed financial model to forecast potential revenue and expenses. I also consult with other departments, such as sales and marketing, to get a better understanding of the potential market demand for the investment opportunity.

By taking a holistic view of the investment opportunity, I am better equipped to make informed decisions and identify any potential roadblocks or challenges."

This answer highlights the candidate's ability to evaluate investment opportunities and demonstrates their understanding of key factors that influence the financial viability of a potential investment.

What to avoid: When answering this question, avoid providing a vague or generic response that does not clearly illustrate your approach and understanding of investment analysis. Refrain from neglecting to mention how you evaluate risks or failing to consider key financial factors. Instead, offer a detailed overview of your investment analysis process, the factors you consider, and how you use this information to make informed decisions.

"How would you define the concept of net present value (NPV)?"

Reason we ask: Your answer to this question should demonstrate your understanding of essential financial concepts and your ability to explain them clearly and concisely. In a corporate finance role, it is crucial to have a strong foundation in financial principles and be able to communicate complex ideas effectively to colleagues and clients.

When asked about the concept of net present value (NPV), it's important to provide a clear and accurate definition while also highlighting its practical applications in investment decision-making. The interviewer may also phrase the question as "What is the significance of NPV in capital budgeting?" or "Why is NPV important in evaluating investment opportunities?" Be prepared to discuss the concept and its relevance in various financial contexts.

Example answer: "Net present value, or NPV, is a financial metric used to evaluate investment opportunities by comparing the present value of cash inflows with the present value of cash outflows. It represents the difference between the present value of future cash flows generated by an investment and the initial cost of the investment. NPV is widely used in capital budgeting to determine the profitability and viability of potential projects. A positive NPV indicates that the expected returns from an investment exceed its cost, making the project worthwhile. Conversely, a negative NPV suggests that the investment would result in a net loss and should be avoided. In essence, NPV helps businesses make informed decisions about which projects to undertake based on their potential to create value for the company."

This answer effectively explains the concept of NPV and its significance in evaluating investment opportunities, demonstrating the candidate's understanding of core financial principles.

What to avoid: When answering this question, avoid providing vague or incomplete explanations that fail to capture the essence of the concept or its applications. Refrain from using jargon or overly technical language without providing adequate context, as this may be perceived as a lack of effective communication skills. Additionally, avoid neglecting the importance of NPV in investment decision-making, as this is a key aspect of its relevance in corporate finance roles.

"How do you know how much debt a company can take on?"

Reason we ask: Your answer to this question should demonstrate your understanding of debt management, financial analysis, and risk assessment, which are crucial skills for a corporate finance role. We want to see that you can evaluate a company's financial situation and make informed recommendations regarding its debt capacity.

When asked about determining how much debt a company can take on, it's important to discuss the key financial metrics and ratios used to assess a company's debt capacity, as well as the qualitative factors that may influence this assessment. The interviewer may also phrase the question as "What factors do you consider when evaluating a company's ability to take on additional debt?" or "How do you assess a company's financial health in relation to its debt capacity?"

Example answer: "To determine how much debt a company can take on, I would start by examining its financial statements and calculating key financial ratios, such as the debt-to-equity ratio, interest coverage ratio, and debt service coverage ratio. These ratios help me understand the company's current debt levels, its ability to generate sufficient cash flow to cover interest payments, and its capacity to repay debt principal.

In addition to these quantitative metrics, I would also consider qualitative factors, such as the company's industry, competitive position, and growth prospects. A company operating in a stable industry with strong growth potential and a competitive advantage may be able to handle a higher level of debt compared to a company facing uncertainties or increased competition. Furthermore, I would evaluate the company's management team, their track record of handling debt, and their strategy for utilizing the additional funds. By combining these quantitative and qualitative factors, I can form a comprehensive assessment of a company's debt capacity and make informed recommendations."

This answer effectively discusses the candidate's approach to determining a company's debt capacity, demonstrating their expertise in financial analysis and risk assessment.

What to avoid: When answering this question, avoid providing a simplistic or one-dimensional approach to evaluating a company's debt capacity, as this may be perceived as a lack of depth in understanding financial analysis and risk management. Additionally, refrain from using jargon or overly technical language without providing adequate context, as this may be perceived as a lack of effective communication skills. Finally, avoid neglecting the importance of qualitative factors in assessing a company's debt capacity, as these can have a significant impact on the overall risk profile.

"How do you ensure accuracy in your work?"

Reason we ask: Your answer to this question should demonstrate your attention to detail, diligence, and commitment to delivering high-quality work, which are essential qualities for a corporate finance role. We want to understand your approach to minimizing errors and ensuring the accuracy of your analyses and recommendations.

When asked about ensuring accuracy in your work, it's important to discuss the specific strategies and practices you use to maintain high standards of accuracy. The interviewer may also phrase the question as "What steps do you take to minimize errors in your financial analysis?" or "How do you maintain the quality of your work in a fast-paced environment?"

Example answer: "To ensure accuracy in my work, I employ a variety of strategies. First, I always start with a clear understanding of the project requirements and objectives, which helps me stay focused on the most relevant data and calculations. I also create detailed checklists for each step of the analysis process, which helps me maintain consistency and avoid overlooking important elements.

In addition to these proactive measures, I regularly double-check my work and cross-reference my calculations with other sources or team members to validate my results. When working with complex financial models, I use built-in error-checking tools to identify potential issues, and I thoroughly test the models under various scenarios to ensure their reliability.

Finally, I believe in fostering a culture of open communication and collaboration within my team. By frequently discussing our work and sharing insights, we can catch any inconsistencies or errors early on, which ultimately contributes to the accuracy and quality of our analyses."

This answer effectively demonstrates the candidate's commitment to accuracy and their proactive approach to maintaining high-quality work.

What to avoid: When answering this question, avoid giving vague or generic responses that don't provide insight into your specific strategies for ensuring accuracy. Additionally, refrain from suggesting that you never make errors or that you solely rely on others to check your work, as this may be perceived as a lack of personal accountability or attention to detail. Finally, avoid focusing only on the technical aspects of accuracy without mentioning the importance of collaboration and communication in maintaining high-quality work.

"What do you know about financial regulations, and how have you applied them in your previous roles?"

Reason we ask: As an entry-level candidate for corporate finance roles, your knowledge and understanding of financial regulations are critical. Your answer will help us assess your awareness of regulatory requirements, your ability to apply them in practical situations, and your potential to develop skills that are essential for success in the corporate finance industry.

When asked about financial regulations, it's essential to demonstrate a basic understanding of regulatory requirements, including the relevant laws, rules, and guidelines. The interviewer may also ask follow-up questions to gauge your familiarity with specific regulations, such as SEC, FINRA, and other regulatory bodies.

Example answer: "Although I am new to the corporate finance industry, I have developed a basic understanding of financial regulations and their importance in ensuring compliance and mitigating risks for organizations. I am familiar with regulations such as the Dodd-Frank Act and Sarbanes-Oxley Act, and I understand the need to comply with relevant regulations to maintain the integrity of financial reporting.

In my previous roles, I have not had direct experience working with financial regulations. However, I have taken courses in financial regulations, participated in mock compliance exercises, and engaged in discussions with professionals in the industry to develop a better understanding of how these regulations impact corporate finance.

As an entry-level candidate, I am eager to learn more about financial regulations and their practical applications in the corporate finance industry. I am willing to work collaboratively with teams to ensure compliance with relevant regulations and mitigate risks for the organization."

This answer demonstrates the candidate's willingness to learn and their basic knowledge of financial regulations. It also highlights their ability to apply their learning from courses, mock compliance exercises, and discussions with industry professionals.

What to avoid: When answering this question, avoid overstating your knowledge or experience with financial regulations. Refrain from providing a vague or generic response that does not demonstrate a basic understanding of regulatory requirements. Also, avoid using technical jargon that may be unfamiliar to the interviewer or over-explaining your knowledge. Instead, offer a concise and straightforward overview of your understanding of financial regulations and your eagerness to learn more about the practical applications of these regulations in the corporate finance industry.

"What are the differences between SEC, FINRA, and other regulatory bodies, and how do they regulate the financial industry?"

Reason we ask: As a candidate for corporate finance roles, it's important to have a basic understanding of the regulatory landscape and the roles played by different regulatory bodies. Your answer to this question will help us assess your knowledge of the financial industry's regulatory framework, your understanding of the differences between regulatory bodies, and your ability to apply regulatory requirements in practice.

When asked about regulatory bodies, it's essential to demonstrate an understanding of their mandates, the scope of their authority, and the specific regulations they enforce. The interviewer may also ask follow-up questions to gauge your familiarity with regulatory requirements, such as those related to securities trading, financial reporting, or investor protection.

Example answer: "SEC and FINRA are two of the primary regulatory bodies that oversee the financial industry in the United States. The SEC is responsible for enforcing federal securities laws, regulating the securities markets, and protecting investors. It oversees the registration of investment advisors, brokers, and other securities professionals, and requires companies to disclose financial and other information to the public.

FINRA, on the other hand, is a self-regulatory organization that oversees securities firms and brokers. It is responsible for enforcing rules related to trading practices, ethical conduct, and investor protection. It also administers licensing exams and provides training for securities professionals.

Other regulatory bodies that are involved in regulating the financial industry include the Federal Reserve, the Commodity

Futures Trading Commission, and state-level regulators. These bodies have varying mandates, but they all play a critical role in ensuring compliance with regulatory requirements and protecting investors.

To comply with these regulatory requirements, companies must maintain detailed records, submit periodic reports, and adhere to specific disclosure requirements. They must also implement internal controls and compliance programs to ensure that their employees are aware of and adhere to relevant regulations."

This answer highlights the candidate's understanding of the differences between regulatory bodies and their mandates. It also demonstrates their awareness of regulatory requirements, such as those related to financial reporting, investor protection, and trading practices.

What to avoid: When answering this question, avoid providing a vague or incomplete response that does not clearly illustrate your understanding of regulatory bodies or their roles. Refrain from focusing solely on one regulatory body or neglecting to mention specific regulations they enforce. Also, avoid using technical jargon that may be unfamiliar to the interviewer. Instead, offer a clear and concise overview of the regulatory landscape, highlighting the differences between regulatory bodies and their mandates.

Interview questions for mid-level corporate finance roles.

"What do you consider to be your greatest strengths and weaknesses as a corporate finance professional?"

Reason we ask: Your answer to this question should demonstrate your self-awareness, as well as your understanding of the skills and qualities required for success in a corporate finance role. We want to know how well you can identify areas of improvement and leverage your strengths to contribute effectively to the company.

When asked about your strengths and weaknesses, it's important to provide balanced and sincere answers. The interviewer may also phrase the question as "What are your greatest assets and areas for improvement as a finance professional?" or "What qualities do you bring to a finance team, and where do you need to grow?"

Example answer: "As a corporate finance professional, one of my key strengths is my analytical ability. I have a strong attention to detail, and I'm skilled at spotting trends and uncovering insights from complex financial data. This has allowed me to make well-informed recommendations and contribute to the overall success of my previous teams.

In terms of weaknesses, I would say that I sometimes struggle with public speaking and presenting my findings to larger groups. While I am confident in my analytical skills, I recognize the importance of effectively communicating my ideas to others. To address this, I've been taking public speaking courses and actively seeking opportunities to practice presenting in front of colleagues. This has helped me become more comfortable and improve my presentation skills, but it's still an area where I can continue to grow."

This answer demonstrates self-awareness and a commitment to professional growth while highlighting a strength that directly relates to the role.

What to avoid: When answering this question, avoid focusing solely on either strengths or weaknesses, as this can create an imbalanced impression. Additionally, refrain from mentioning weaknesses that are critical to the role or presenting strengths as weaknesses, as this may come across as insincere. It's essential to choose actual professional strengths and weaknesses that are relevant to the corporate finance field and to demonstrate your commitment to addressing areas for improvement.

"How do you approach budgeting and cost control, and what methods do you use to ensure financial discipline?"

Reason we ask: When responding to this question, it's important to showcase your experience in budgeting and cost control, along with your proficiency in implementing effective financial discipline methods. Providing this information will help us gain insights into your capabilities and determine your suitability for a mid-level corporate finance role. Moreover, your answer will give us an idea of whether you were more tactical or strategic in your previous positions.

It's asked about your approach to budgeting and cost control, it's important to be specific and provide examples of the methods you use. The interviewer may also phrase the question as "What strategies have you employed to maintain budgets and control costs?" or "Can you share examples of how you've ensured financial discipline in your previous roles?"

Example answer: "In my previous corporate finance roles, I have approached budgeting and cost control by thoroughly analyzing historical financial data and using it to create realistic and flexible budgets. I also involve key stakeholders in the budgeting process to ensure buy-in and alignment across departments. To maintain cost control, I implement regular monitoring and reporting of actual expenses against budget, which helps identify variances early and allows for timely corrective actions.

To ensure financial discipline, I use tools such as variance analysis and forecasting to help identify trends and potential issues. I also establish clear communication channels and encourage open dialogue with team members and other departments, promoting a culture of financial accountability. Additionally, I prioritize continuous improvement by regularly reviewing processes and seeking opportunities for cost savings or efficiency gains."

This answer demonstrates a comprehensive understanding of budgeting and cost control while highlighting the candidate's experience and ability to apply various methods for financial discipline.

What to avoid: When answering this question, avoid providing vague or generic responses that do not demonstrate your understanding of budgeting and cost control. Also, refrain from discussing methods unrelated to corporate finance, as this may create confusion about your experience and expertise. Instead, focus on specific techniques and examples that showcase your skills and experience in managing budgets and controlling costs in a corporate finance context.

"What do you know about Trade Finance? Which products are the most relevant in your opinion?"

Reason we ask: Your answer to this question should demonstrate your understanding of trade finance and its various products. This will help us gauge your expertise and knowledge in this area, which is essential for a mid-level corporate finance role.

When asked about trade finance, it's important to showcase your understanding of the topic and highlight the most relevant products based on your experience or industry trends. The interviewer may also phrase the question as "Can you explain the concept of trade finance and discuss the most important products in this area?" or "How would you rank trade finance products in terms of importance and relevance to businesses?"

Example answer: "Trade finance refers to the financial instruments and products that facilitate international trade and commerce by mitigating risks associated with cross-border transactions. Some of the key trade finance products include letters of credit, which provide a guarantee of payment between a buyer and seller; documentary collections, which involve the exchange of documents between banks on behalf of the trading parties; and various forms of guarantees and standby letters of credit, which can be used to secure performance or financial obligations.

In my opinion, letters of credit are one of the most relevant trade finance products, as they offer a high level of security for both the buyer and seller by involving banks as intermediaries. Additionally, trade finance insurance products are becoming increasingly important, as they help mitigate credit and political risks in international trade, particularly in emerging markets."

This answer demonstrates a solid understanding of trade finance and highlights specific products based on their relevance and importance to businesses.

What to avoid: When answering this question, avoid providing a superficial or incomplete explanation of trade finance, as this may create doubts about your knowledge and expertise. Additionally, refrain from discussing products that are unrelated to trade finance or providing opinions that are not backed up by industry trends or personal experience. Instead, focus on providing a clear and concise explanation of trade finance and its most relevant products based on your experience or current market trends.

"How do you approach financial forecasting and planning, and what factors do you consider when making projections?"

Reason we ask: Your answer to this question should demonstrate your understanding of financial forecasting and planning, and your ability to consider various factors when making projections. This is essential for a mid-level corporate finance role, as accurate forecasting and planning are critical for a company's financial success.

When asked about financial forecasting and planning, it's important to showcase your approach to this critical task and highlight the factors you consider when making projections. The interviewer may also phrase the question as "Can you explain your methodology for financial forecasting and planning?" or

"What are the key elements you take into account when creating financial projections?"

Example answer: "When approaching financial forecasting and planning, I start by analyzing historical financial data to identify trends and patterns. I then consider external factors such as market conditions, industry trends, and economic indicators that may impact the company's performance. Additionally, I collaborate with various departments to gather input on their expectations and plans, which helps create a more comprehensive forecast.

When making projections, I consider factors such as sales growth, changes in operating expenses, and potential capital investments. I also account for any upcoming product launches, expansion plans, or other strategic initiatives that might affect the company's financial performance. To ensure accuracy, I continually update the forecast as new information becomes available and monitor actual performance against projections, making adjustments as needed."

This answer demonstrates a structured approach to financial forecasting and planning and highlights the various factors considered when making projections.

What to avoid: When answering this question, avoid providing a vague or superficial explanation of your approach, as this may create doubts about your knowledge and expertise. Additionally, refrain from focusing solely on quantitative aspects without considering qualitative factors or ignoring the importance of collaboration with other departments. Instead, focus on providing a clear and comprehensive explanation of your approach to financial forecasting and planning, showcasing your ability to consider multiple factors and collaborate with other stakeholders in the process.

"How do you collaborate with business partners and stakeholders to ensure alignment between financial plans and business objectives?"

Reason we ask: Collaboration is critical in executive-level corporate finance roles, and your ability to work effectively with business partners and stakeholders is crucial for success. Your answer to this question will help us assess your approach to collaboration, your ability to align financial plans with business objectives, and your capacity to drive results through cross-functional teamwork.

When asked about collaboration with business partners and stakeholders, it's essential to provide a comprehensive overview of your approach, highlighting the key principles, methods, and tools you employ. The interviewer may also ask follow-up questions to gauge your experience in managing complex business relationships and driving alignment between financial plans and business objectives.

Example answer: "Collaboration is a key component of my approach to corporate finance, and I believe in working closely with business partners and stakeholders to ensure that financial plans align with business objectives. To achieve this alignment, I first seek to understand the goals and objectives of each department and function, as well as the overall business strategy.

I then work with cross-functional teams to develop financial plans that support these goals and objectives, using both financial and non-financial metrics to assess progress and ensure alignment. I also make sure to communicate regularly with business partners and stakeholders, providing regular updates on financial performance and seeking input and feedback on how to improve.

To drive results through collaboration, I place a strong emphasis on building and maintaining relationships based on trust, respect, and open communication. By working together towards shared objectives, we can achieve better financial performance and overall business success."

This answer demonstrates the candidate's strategic approach to collaboration, their ability to align financial plans with business objectives, and their capacity to drive results through cross-functional teamwork.

What to avoid: When answering this question, avoid providing a generic response that does not clearly illustrate your approach to collaboration and alignment between financial plans and business objectives. Refrain from neglecting the importance of communication and relationship-building in driving cross-functional teamwork. Also, avoid focusing solely on financial metrics and neglecting non-financial metrics. Instead, offer a detailed overview of your approach to collaboration, the strategies and tools you use, and specific examples of how you have managed complex business relationships and driven alignment between financial plans and business objectives while achieving business success.

"Have you ever had to deal with a difficult financial situation or challenge in your work? How did you handle it?"

Reason we ask: Your answer to this question should provide insight into your problem-solving skills, adaptability, and ability to handle challenging financial situations in a corporate finance role. This will help us gauge your ability to navigate complexities and find solutions in high-pressure environments.

When asked about dealing with a difficult financial situation or challenge, it's important to be specific and provide a clear example of the situation you faced, the actions you took to resolve it, and the outcome. The interviewer may also phrase the question as "Can you give an example of a time when you faced a financial challenge at work?" or "How do you tackle complex financial problems in your role?"

Example answer: "In my previous role as a Financial Analyst, I encountered a situation where our company faced a sudden cash flow shortage due to delayed payments from a major client. This put significant strain on our working capital, and we needed to find a solution quickly to meet our short-term financial obligations.

I worked closely with the finance team to analyze our current cash position, upcoming expenses, and potential sources of short-term financing. We decided to negotiate an extension on some of our payables and implemented stricter credit terms for new clients to minimize the risk of future cash flow issues. Additionally, I suggested setting up a revolving credit facility to provide a financial cushion for unexpected situations. These measures helped us navigate the cash flow crunch and implement more robust financial controls to prevent similar issues in the future."

This answer demonstrates the candidate's ability to analyze a complex financial situation, collaborate with a team, and develop effective solutions.

What to avoid: When answering this question, avoid providing a vague or generic response that does not showcase your problem-solving abilities. Refrain from blaming others for the financial challenge or portraying yourself as the sole hero in the situation. Instead, focus on providing a detailed account of the situation, your thought process, the actions you took, and the lessons learned, emphasizing your ability to collaborate and adapt to challenging financial situations.

"Can you share an example of a situation where you had to navigate a complex regulatory landscape to achieve a business objective?"

Reason we ask: As a mid-level candidate for corporate finance roles, you are expected to have experience in navigating complex regulatory landscapes and identifying strategies to achieve business objectives while complying with regulatory requirements. Your answer to this question will help us assess your ability to apply regulatory knowledge in practice, your problem-solving skills, and your capacity to work collaboratively with cross-functional teams.

When asked about navigating complex regulatory landscapes, it's essential to provide a detailed overview of the situation, the specific regulatory requirements involved, and the strategies you employed to achieve the business objective. The interviewer may also ask follow-up questions to gauge your understanding of regulatory requirements, such as those related to financial reporting, risk management, or investor protection.

Example answer: "In my previous role, we were pursuing a business objective that involved expanding into a new market, which was subject to specific regulatory requirements related to licensing and compliance. The regulatory landscape was complex and constantly evolving, and it required us to work collaboratively with cross-functional teams to navigate it successfully.

To achieve our business objective, we first conducted an in-depth analysis of the regulatory landscape to identify the specific requirements we needed to meet. We then developed a comprehensive compliance program that included policies, procedures, and training programs to ensure that all employees understood their responsibilities under the relevant regulations.

We also engaged with regulators to seek guidance and input on our compliance program, which helped us identify areas of improvement and build strong relationships with regulatory authorities. Additionally, we worked closely with our legal team to ensure that all necessary approvals and permits were obtained, and that we were in compliance with all relevant regulations.

By taking a proactive and collaborative approach to navigating the regulatory landscape, we were able to achieve our business objective while maintaining compliance with regulatory requirements."

This answer demonstrates the candidate's ability to navigate complex regulatory landscapes, work collaboratively with cross-functional teams, and identify strategies to achieve business objectives while complying with regulatory requirements.

What to avoid: When answering this question, avoid providing a vague or generic response that does not clearly illustrate the complexity of the regulatory landscape or the specific regulatory requirements involved. Refrain from focusing solely on the business objective without providing details on how you navigated the regulatory landscape. Also, avoid taking sole credit for success without acknowledging the contributions of cross-functional teams or legal counsel. Instead, offer a detailed and specific example of a complex regulatory landscape you navigated, the regulatory requirements involved, and the strategies you employed to achieve the business objective while maintaining compliance with regulatory requirements.

"How do you ensure compliance with regulatory requirements in your work, and what strategies have you found to be most effective?"

Reason we ask: As a mid-level candidate for corporate finance roles, your ability to ensure compliance with regulatory requirements is critical. Your answer to this question will help us assess your understanding of regulatory requirements, your ability to develop and implement compliance programs, and your capacity to manage risks and mitigate non-compliance issues.

When asked about ensuring compliance with regulatory requirements, it's essential to provide a comprehensive overview of your approach, highlighting the key principles, methods, and tools you employ. The interviewer may also ask follow-up questions to gauge your familiarity with specific regulatory requirements, such as those related to financial reporting, risk management, or investor protection.

Example answer: "In my previous roles, I have developed a proactive and comprehensive approach to ensuring compliance with regulatory requirements. I start by developing a deep understanding of the specific regulatory requirements relevant to the business or project, including laws, rules, and guidelines.

I then develop a compliance program that includes policies, procedures, and training programs to ensure that all employees understand their responsibilities under the relevant regulations. I also work closely with cross-functional teams, including legal counsel and external auditors, to identify areas of non-compliance and develop corrective action plans to address them.

To ensure ongoing compliance, I implement regular reporting and analysis of compliance metrics, including the identification of key risk areas and trends. I also work to maintain open and transparent communication with regulators and other stakeholders to ensure that we are aware of any changes in regulatory requirements and can adjust our compliance programs accordingly.

Overall, I believe that a proactive and collaborative approach to compliance is essential for mitigating risks and ensuring compliance with regulatory requirements."

This answer demonstrates the candidate's proactive approach to ensuring compliance, their ability to develop and implement compliance programs, and their capacity to manage risks and mitigate non-compliance issues.

What to avoid: When answering this question, avoid providing a vague or generic response that does not clearly illustrate your approach to ensuring compliance with regulatory requirements. Refrain from focusing solely on the development of compliance programs without providing specific examples of how you identify and address areas of non-compliance. Also, avoid over-explaining regulatory requirements or using technical jargon that may be unfamiliar to the interviewer. Instead, offer a detailed overview of your approach to ensuring compliance, the strategies and tools you use, and specific examples of how you have managed risks and mitigated non-compliance issues.

Interview questions for senior and executive-level corporate finance roles.

"Can you discuss a time when you had to lead a large-scale financial transformation or change initiative, and what steps you took to ensure success?"

Reason we ask: Your answer to this question should demonstrate your ability to lead significant financial projects, navigate complexities, and drive successful outcomes. This will help us assess your strategic thinking, leadership skills, and capacity to manage large-scale initiatives in a VP or executive-level corporate finance role.

When asked about leading a large-scale financial transformation or change initiative, it's crucial to provide a clear example of the project, the challenges you faced, your leadership approach, and the outcomes. The interviewer may also phrase the question as "Tell me about a time when you successfully managed a major financial project" or "What was your strategy for implementing a significant financial change in your organization?"

Example answer: "In my previous role as a CFO, I was tasked with leading a company-wide financial transformation to improve profitability and streamline our financial processes. This involved evaluating our entire cost structure, identifying inefficiencies, and implementing new financial systems and controls.

First, I formed a cross-functional team with representatives from various departments to ensure all perspectives were considered. We conducted a thorough analysis of our current processes, identified areas for improvement, and developed a comprehensive plan to address these issues. This plan included renegotiating contracts, consolidating vendors, and implementing new financial software to automate and standardize processes.

Throughout the project, I maintained open communication with stakeholders, providing regular updates and soliciting feedback. This ensured alignment and buy-in from all parties involved. The transformation resulted in a 15% reduction in operating expenses and significantly improved the efficiency of our financial processes."

This answer showcases the candidate's strategic thinking, leadership, and ability to deliver successful outcomes in a complex financial project.

What to avoid: When answering this question, avoid providing a generic or vague response that does not demonstrate your ability to lead large-scale financial projects. Refrain from taking full credit for the success of the initiative, as this may come across as arrogant. Instead, focus on providing a detailed account of the project, your leadership approach, the collaboration with your team, and the outcomes achieved, emphasizing your ability to drive change and create lasting impact.

"How would you finance an NPA asset?"

Reason we ask: Your answer to this question should demonstrate your knowledge of non-performing assets (NPAs), your strategic thinking, and your ability to analyze and evaluate different financing options. This will help us assess your capabilities in managing complex financial situations and making informed decisions in a VP or executive-level corporate finance role.

When asked about financing an NPA asset, it's crucial to provide a thoughtful response that outlines your understanding of the challenges associated with NPAs, the factors you would consider, and the potential strategies for financing. The interviewer may also phrase the question as "What approach would you take to address the financing of a non-performing asset?" or "Can you discuss your strategy for managing non-performing assets in a financial portfolio?"

Example answer: "When dealing with an NPA asset, it's essential to first analyze the reasons behind its non-performance and assess the potential for recovery. Depending on the findings, different financing options can be considered.

If the asset has the potential for turnaround with appropriate restructuring, we could explore options like refinancing or rescheduling the debt, converting debt to equity, or bringing in strategic partners. It's crucial to work closely with the borrower to develop a mutually beneficial plan that increases the likelihood of recovery.

In cases where the asset's recovery is less likely, we may consider disposing of the asset through an asset sale, partnering with an asset reconstruction company, or exploring a debt-for-assets swap. The key is to minimize losses and maximize value recovery while mitigating risks.

Regardless of the chosen strategy, it's essential to involve all stakeholders, maintain open communication, and monitor the progress of the financing plan to ensure its success."

This answer showcases the candidate's knowledge of NPAs, strategic thinking, and ability to evaluate different financing options while considering the risks and potential for recovery.

What to avoid: When answering this question, avoid providing a one-size-fits-all solution or a generic response that does not demonstrate your understanding of the complexities involved in financing an NPA asset. Refrain from oversimplifying the issue or suggesting a single approach without considering the specific circumstances of the asset. Instead, focus on providing a thoughtful analysis of the factors that would influence your decision-making and discussing various potential strategies based on the asset's recovery potential.

"What type of roles have you supported in your past positions?"

Reason we ask: Your answer to this question should provide insight into your experience, the breadth and depth of your expertise, and your ability to support various roles and functions within an organization. This information will help us determine if your background aligns with the needs of a VP or executive-level corporate finance role and if you have the skills and knowledge necessary to succeed in this position.

When asked about the roles you have supported in your past positions, it's essential to provide a comprehensive overview of your experience, highlighting the key functions and areas in which you have worked. The interviewer may also phrase the question as "Can you discuss the different roles and responsibilities you have had in your previous positions?" or "How has your past experience prepared you for a VP or executive-level corporate finance role?"

Example answer: "Throughout my career, I have had the opportunity to support various roles within finance and corporate strategy. I started as a Financial Analyst, where I gained experience in budgeting, forecasting, and financial reporting. Later, I transitioned into a Finance Manager role, overseeing a team responsible for financial planning and analysis.

In my most recent role as a Director of Finance, I collaborated with executive leadership and cross-functional teams to develop and implement strategic initiatives aimed at driving growth, reducing costs, and optimizing financial performance. I also played a critical role in mergers and acquisitions, due diligence, and post-merger integration activities.

These experiences have provided me with a deep understanding of the complexities of corporate finance and equipped me with the skills necessary to excel in a VP or executive-level role."

This answer highlights the candidate's diverse experience and demonstrates their ability to support various roles and functions within an organization.

What to avoid: When answering this question, avoid providing a vague or generic response that does not clearly illustrate your experience and expertise. Refrain from focusing solely on your most recent role or neglecting to mention key areas of responsibility. Instead, offer a detailed overview of your professional background, emphasizing the roles you have supported, the responsibilities you have held, and how these experiences have prepared you for a VP or executive-level corporate finance role.

"How do you think about and manage financial performance, and what metrics or KPIs do you use to assess success?"

Reason we ask: Your answer to this question should provide insight into your approach to managing financial performance, your understanding of key metrics and KPIs, and your ability to evaluate and drive success within an organization. This information will help us determine if your financial management style aligns with the needs of a VP or executive-level corporate finance role and if you have the skills and knowledge necessary to succeed in this position.

When asked about managing financial performance and the metrics or KPIs you use to assess success, it's essential to provide a comprehensive overview of your approach, highlighting the key principles, methods, and tools you employ. The interviewer may also phrase the question as "What is your approach to financial performance management, and how do you measure success?" or "Can you discuss the financial metrics and KPIs that are most important to you and your approach to financial management?"

Example answer: "When it comes to managing financial performance, I believe in a balanced and proactive approach that involves setting clear objectives, monitoring progress, and adjusting strategies as needed. I use a combination of financial and non-financial metrics to assess success and drive decision-making.

Some of the key financial KPIs I focus on include revenue growth, gross margin, EBITDA margin, and return on investment (ROI). I also consider non-financial metrics, such as customer satisfaction and employee engagement, as these can have a significant impact on financial performance.

To ensure success, I implement regular reporting and analysis of these KPIs, and I work closely with cross-functional teams to identify areas of improvement and develop action plans to address any issues. By maintaining a holistic view of the organization's performance, I am better equipped to drive growth and profitability."

This answer highlights the candidate's strategic approach to financial performance management and demonstrates their understanding of key metrics and KPIs.

What to avoid: When answering this question, avoid providing a vague or generic response that does not clearly illustrate your approach and understanding of financial performance management. Refrain from focusing solely on one or two KPIs or neglecting to mention how you use these metrics to drive decision-making and success. Instead, offer a detailed overview of your approach to managing financial performance, the metrics and KPIs you use to assess success, and how these tools inform your decision-making and strategy development.

"How do you balance the need to comply with financial regulations with the need to achieve business objectives and remain competitive in the market?"

Reason we ask: As a senior or executive-level candidate for corporate finance roles, you are expected to have extensive experience in navigating complex regulatory landscapes while simultaneously driving business growth and maintaining competitiveness in the market. Your answer to this question will help us assess your ability to manage competing priorities, your strategic thinking skills, and your capacity to lead cross-functional teams to achieve regulatory compliance and business objectives.

When asked about balancing the need for compliance with regulatory requirements and business objectives, it's essential to provide a comprehensive overview of your approach, highlighting the key principles, methods, and tools you employ. The interviewer may also ask follow-up questions to gauge your experience in managing competing priorities and leading cross-functional teams.

Example answer: "Balancing regulatory compliance with business objectives and market competitiveness is a critical challenge that I have navigated throughout my career. I believe that the key to success is to take a proactive and strategic approach to compliance, while at the same time driving business growth and innovation.

To achieve this balance, I start by developing a deep understanding of the regulatory landscape and the specific regulatory requirements relevant to the business objectives. I then work collaboratively with cross-functional teams to identify areas of non-compliance, develop corrective action plans, and ensure ongoing compliance with regulatory requirements.

At the same time, I also focus on driving business growth and innovation by seeking out new opportunities and developing strategies that align with the regulatory landscape. This requires a comprehensive understanding of the market, competitive forces, and emerging trends, as well as the ability to lead cross-functional teams to execute on strategic initiatives.

Ultimately, the key to balancing regulatory compliance with business objectives and market competitiveness is to maintain a strategic focus and work collaboratively with cross-functional teams to achieve both compliance and business objectives."

This answer demonstrates the candidate's ability to manage competing priorities, their strategic thinking skills, and their capacity to lead cross-functional teams to achieve regulatory compliance and business objectives.

What to avoid: When answering this question, avoid providing a vague or generic response that does not clearly illustrate your approach to balancing regulatory compliance with business objectives and market competitiveness. Refrain from focusing solely on compliance or business objectives without providing specific examples of how you balance both priorities. Also, avoid neglecting the importance of cross-functional collaboration and leadership in achieving both compliance and business objectives. Instead, offer a detailed overview of your strategic approach to balancing regulatory compliance with business objectives and market competitiveness, the strategies and tools you use, and specific examples of how you have managed competing priorities while driving business growth and maintaining regulatory compliance.

"How do you handle situations where you suspect a colleague or business partner may be in violation of a financial regulation?"

Reason we ask: As a candidate for corporate finance roles, your ability to identify and report potential violations of financial regulations is critical. Your answer to this question will help us assess your understanding of regulatory requirements, your ethical standards, and your capacity to manage risks and maintain compliance with regulatory requirements.

When asked about handling situations where you suspect a colleague or business partner may be in violation of a financial regulation, it's essential to provide a comprehensive overview of your approach, highlighting the key principles, methods, and tools you employ. The interviewer may also ask follow-up questions to gauge your experience in managing ethical dilemmas and reporting potential violations of financial regulations.

Example answer: "Maintaining compliance with financial regulations is critical to the success and reputation of the organization. If I suspect that a colleague or business partner may be in violation of a financial regulation, I take the matter very seriously and follow a defined process to address it.

First, I review the specific regulatory requirements involved to determine whether a violation has occurred. If I believe a violation has occurred, I raise the issue with my supervisor or the appropriate compliance officer in the organization, as well as any legal counsel or regulatory authority as necessary.

I also ensure that I maintain detailed records of the situation and any actions taken, to ensure that there is a clear audit trail and that the issue is resolved appropriately. If the violation is related to a colleague, I communicate the issue in a professional and respectful manner, making it clear that I am raising the issue in the interest of regulatory compliance and the organization's reputation.

Ultimately, my approach is guided by a commitment to ethical behavior and regulatory compliance, and I believe that by raising potential violations of financial regulations, we can maintain a strong compliance culture and protect the organization's reputation."

This answer demonstrates the candidate's commitment to ethical behavior and regulatory compliance, their ability to follow defined processes to address potential violations of financial regulations, and their capacity to manage risks and maintain compliance with regulatory requirements.

What to avoid: When answering this question, avoid providing a vague or generic response that does not clearly illustrate your approach to handling situations where you suspect a colleague or business partner may be in violation of a financial regulation. Refrain from neglecting the importance of following defined processes and maintaining detailed records. Also, avoid taking unilateral action without first consulting with supervisors or appropriate compliance officers. Instead, offer a detailed overview of your approach to handling potential violations of financial regulations, the strategies and tools you use, and specific examples of how you have managed ethical dilemmas and reported potential violations of financial regulations while protecting the organization's reputation.

The Do's and Don'ts of Interviewing

There are a few key factors that can make or break your success in any interview process. To help you out, I've put together a list of these factors for you to review and keep in mind.

Things that you should do if you want to be more successful in your interviews.

Do thorough research before your interview.

To succeed in the interview, you need to prepare yourself by doing thorough research. Start by gathering as much information as possible about the company, their mission, and how the position you are interviewing for will contribute to achieving their goals. Additionally, familiarize yourself with the industry and who their main competitors are. To prepare for the specific job, study the job description, identify what qualities the ideal candidate should have, and think of ways to highlight your strengths that align with those qualities. It is also beneficial to conduct social media research on the interviewers, as this can provide valuable insights into their background and interests. By learning about them, you can also prepare thoughtful questions to ask during the interview.

Prepare in advance.

Try to plan and prepare for your interview in advance so that you don't feel rushed or stressed out. It's essential to stay calm and relaxed in the hours leading up to your interview. Take some time to unwind and listen to something uplifting that puts you in a positive state of mind. Strive to be professional, but also friendly and approachable, as the hiring team will be evaluating your personality and attitude as well as your qualifications and experience.

Dress for the job you are interviewing for.

When preparing for your interview, consider the dress code for the job you want, and aim to dress at least one level above that standard. Remember, the version of you that the interviewer sees during the interview should be your best self. Dressing inappropriately, such as wearing jeans and a t-shirt to an interview for a business-casual job, shows a lack of understanding and interest in the position.

Focus on your accomplishments more than your duties.

As previously discussed in this book, the answers you provide during an interview hold a hierarchy of impressiveness. While a candidate may possess all the necessary skills for the job, providing weak answers can still leave a negative impression on the interviewer.

Include transferable skills if you are newly graduated or doing a career change.

If you do not have direct accomplishments or experience, use things that you have done that transfer well to the profile.

Express interest and enthusiasm for the opportunity.

A common mistake that candidates make is not being sure if they genuinely want the position, and this lack of commitment shows in their demeanor during the interview. If you are interviewing for a job, it is important to convey your interest in the position and make a positive impression. Ultimately, you want the decision to be yours to make. If you are offered the job and decide it is not the right career move, that is okay, as it will be your decision. However, if you come across as indifferent during the interview, the interviewer may decide that you are not the right fit for the job. Towards the end of the interview, show your interest by asking about the next steps and expressing what you like about the company and the opportunity.

Have good eye-contact and body language.

Showing lack of presence during an interview indicates a lack of interest, enthusiasm, and professionalism. This type of behavior can hinder your chances of being hired, as employers prefer candidates who show genuine interest and enthusiasm. Being disinterested and indifferent may suggest that you are only looking for a short-term position and not committed to doing high-quality work. So, it is crucial to stay engaged and present throughout the interview to make a positive impression.

Listen carefully to each question, even clarify what the interviewer is asking if needed.

Being mentally present during an interview is crucial for a candidate to succeed. It's common to get lost in your own thoughts and focus on what you're going to say next, but failing to pay attention to the interviewer's question can result in a poor answer. This not only reflects a lack of listening skills but also shows a lack of interest in the job and the interview process. To avoid this mistake, listen carefully to the question and take a moment to gather your thoughts before answering.

Answer all questions but use Answer/Ask.

The most impressive candidates are often those who exude a relaxed and confident demeanor during interviews. This book can help you achieve that. A candidate who engages in a back-and-forth conversation with the interviewer is more memorable than those who simply answer questions. When you ask questions, make sure they are relevant to the topic at hand. For example, if the interviewer asks about your preferred technology, you can answer and follow up by asking the interviewer about their preferences. Practice this technique of answering and then asking with someone beforehand and aim to use it about thirty percent of the time. This approach not only makes you stand out from other candidates, but it also helps you learn more about the job opportunity.

Example: Interviewer asks you *"What CRM software do you have experience with?"* and you respond with *"I have worked mostly with Salesforce, HubSpot, and Keap. What CRM do you use here and how do you like it?"*

Practice before your interview.

Rather than memorizing your answers, practice articulating your main points confidently. A helpful technique is recording yourself leaving your answers in your own voicemail and then listening to them later for self-reflection. Alternatively, consider finding a friend or colleague to conduct "mock interviews" with you. One effective exercise is to play the role of the interviewer and ask questions based on the ideal candidate profile to determine whether they would be a good fit. Through this process, you can gain valuable insights into areas you need to improve upon in your own answers.

Send a thank you email or note after every interview.

Sending a thank you note after your interview is a great way to show your appreciation and leave a positive impression. It is recommended to send the thank you note within 24 hours of the interview or one day before the interviewer makes their decision if they have specified a date. An email is usually the best way to send the note, but if the industry is more personal, a physical note may be more appropriate. If you do not have the interviewer's email, you can send it to the recruiter and ask them to forward it to the interviewer on your behalf.

Follow-up thank you email/notes should be short, typically 3-4 sentences long and should include:

1. Thank the interviewer for their time.

2. Remind them of the top 1 or 2 things about your fit for the job that you believe impressed them.

3. If needed, try to mitigate any concerns about your fit with the job that they expressed. (One sentence.)

4. Convey interest in moving forward with the interview process or receiving an offer for the job.

Accept that this is a process, and you will not get every job that you want.

Perseverance is key in the job interview process. Even if you have a less than perfect interview, it is important to stay positive and learn from your mistakes. Take an honest look at your performance and make small adjustments to improve your approach. It can be challenging, but keeping a positive attitude is essential for success.

I recall working with a recent college graduate who had no professional experience, but was determined to become a pharmaceutical sales representative. She had some social awkwardness but was likable and eager to learn. While she was not a top candidate, I believed in her and arranged for her to interview with two of my clients. Despite not receiving an offer, she persevered and continued to interview on her own. Eventually, she landed a job with a major company and has spent over two decades in her desired career. With each interview, she gained more confidence and improved her approach.

Remember to stay persistent, remain positive, and keep working at it. Even if you face rejection or setbacks, every interview is a learning opportunity to help you become a better candidate.

Things that you should avoid if you want to be more successful in your interviews:

Forgetting something.

Allow yourself ample time to prepare for your interview. This will help you avoid any last-minute mishaps and ensure that you do not forget anything important. Before your interview, the hiring manager may request that you review specific information, complete a questionnaire, or undertake an assignment. Make sure you have completed all these tasks before your interview. It is important to double- and triple-check everything to ensure you don't miss anything important.

Arriving late.

When it comes to face-to-face interviews, it's best to arrive at the location ten to fifteen minutes before your scheduled interview time. However, for phone or video interviews, make sure to be ready three to five minutes before the scheduled time, whether it's logging in to a video platform or having your phone nearby and fully charged.

No call/no show.

Failing to show up for your interview without any notice, especially through a phone call, is a surefire way to miss out on a job opportunity. It can have a long-lasting negative impact on your reputation, not only for the job in question but also for future opportunities. This kind of behavior is unprofessional and can lead to a lasting negative impression, which may harm your chances of securing the position you desire."

Sounding as though your answers are just rehearsed words you think you are supposed to say.

Although it is important to prepare for expected interview questions, it is equally important to avoid appearing too rehearsed. Instead of memorizing responses word-for-word, focus on bullet points you want to cover in your answers.

Practicing ahead of time is helpful, but try to strike a balance between preparedness and spontaneity. Being sincere and relaxed during the interview will go a long way in impressing your interviewer.

Leave your phone volume on during the interview.

Although it may seem like a small detail, forgetting to silence your phone during an interview can have a negative impact on your candidacy. While it may not be a dealbreaker, it could make a difference if another candidate is equally qualified. It may come across as unprofessional and suggest that you lack attention to detail. Therefore, make sure to double-check that your phone is silenced before the interview to avoid any potential distractions or interruptions.

Speaking negatively about previous jobs.

When interviewing for a job, it's important to maintain a positive attitude and avoid speaking negatively about previous employers or colleagues. Complaining or gossiping may lead the interviewer to perceive you as a toxic ex-employee. Instead, focus on your accomplishments, objectives, and connections. If asked about a bad experience, frame it as a learning opportunity. Highlight your interest in the new company and how your skills and experiences align with their goals. This positive approach will make you a more attractive candidate and increase your chances of success.

Being arrogant or rude to anyone.

It's crucial to be courteous and friendly to everyone you encounter while interviewing at a company. Remember, the interviewer might ask for feedback from any staff member you interacted with during your visit. Therefore, it's crucial to be polite and kind to all employees, from the receptionist to the janitor. It's also an excellent opportunity to demonstrate your interpersonal skills, as being pleasant and engaging with people you meet can give the interviewer a positive impression of you.

Being dishonest.

Lying or even appearing dishonest can be an automatic dealbreaker, even if you have all the qualifications. Employers have ways of verifying information, and if they find out you've lied, it's game over. Even if you somehow manage to get hired, any dishonesty that is later uncovered can lead to termination. It's always better to be honest, even if it means admitting a weakness or a lack of experience in a certain area.

Delay in responding to recruiters or hiring managers.

Feedback is crucial after an interview with someone besides the recruiter. Hiring managers and recruiters may also request clarification on something you mentioned during an interview. Failing to provide timely responses or withholding information gives the impression that you are not motivated to get the job. It is important to provide requested information promptly and with transparency.

Over-explaining.

When answering interview questions, it's important to be concise and to the point. A good rule of thumb is to keep your responses to about thirty to sixty seconds. If your answer goes over ninety seconds, it may be too long and lose the interviewer's attention. Try to avoid meandering or rambling answers. If the interviewer wants more detail or clarification, they will ask follow-up questions. Remember to be concise and clear while still answering the question that is being asked.

Giving vague answers.

When answering interview questions, make sure to provide specific examples to support your responses. Vague answers can come across as evasive, and can give the impression that you are trying to hide something or are not being truthful. Remember, the interviewer is trying to assess your skills and experience, so providing concrete examples helps to demonstrate your qualifications and build credibility. Avoid giving general or overly broad responses, and instead provide details that highlight your strengths and accomplishments.

Demonstrating a lack of taking responsibility.

When discussing past mistakes, avoid blaming others. During an interview, you may be asked to talk about a time when you made a mistake at work. It's important to take ownership of your actions and avoid placing the blame solely on your colleagues. Claiming that you've never made a mistake may come across as insincere. Instead, talk about what you learned from the mistake and how you would handle the situation differently if it were to happen again.

Don't get the most out of your time.

It's important to remember that interviews are not just about answering questions but also about asking them. If you only focus on answering questions and do not ask any, it can leave a negative impression on the interviewer. Research the company beforehand and prepare a list of questions to ask. Use these to guide you during the interview, or when it feels appropriate to use the Answer/Ask technique. Most interviewers will leave time at the end of the interview for you to ask questions, so be sure to take advantage of this opportunity. Asking good questions demonstrates your interest in the job and can give you an advantage over other candidates. For more information on the best questions to ask, check out the chapter titled 'Best Questions That Candidates Ask the Interviewer'.

Being unprofessional.

It's essential to maintain proper posture during the interview and avoid fidgeting with your hands or feet or any items around you. An interviewer once shared with me a story about a candidate who put their feet up on a chair during the interview, and another who was chewing gum. While these may seem like minor issues, they can create a negative impression. Keep in mind that during an interview, you are expected to be at your best, and anything less may lead the interviewer to wonder how you might behave as an employee. To avoid such mishaps, it's best to maintain a professional demeanor throughout the interview process.

Give a bad impression of your personality.

When interviewing for a job, be aware that certain personality traits may lead the interviewer to screen you out of the hiring process. Although interviewers do not explicitly test you for these traits, their experience in hiring informs them on how these traits can lead to problematic hires. These traits come up in discussions with hiring managers and impact the decision-making process. This is especially true for startups where smaller teams require employees to work closely with each other. While you cannot change your personality, it is important to be self-aware and avoid projecting these traits.

Top personality traits that interviewers watch out for.

1. Overly self-absorbed.
2. Dishonest/untrustworthy.
3. Inability to take responsibility for mistakes, especially by blaming others.
4. Inflexible and not open to new ideas, suggestions, or coaching. (I would include the "know-it-all" candidates in this category.)
5. Fragile ego that is unable to process constructive criticism.
6. Reckless risk taking. (Calculated risk taking is great, but careless actions are not.)
7. Bitter/angry or anything else that might indicate a future toxic co-worker/employee.

It's essential to treat every interaction with any company employee as a type of interview. Candidates might perform well in the interview with the hiring manager but fail to get the job because of a negative impression from the receptionist or anyone else they interact with. It's also important to keep up your professional demeanor in every meeting or conversation, even if it's a casual one. A moment of letting your guard down and saying something inappropriate can jeopardize your chances of getting hired. Always remember that every interaction is a chance to make a positive impression and be considered for the position.

How to Stand Out from Others

The employer's selection process is like a funnel, with numerous candidates entering at the top, and fewer progressing through each stage. As you move through the process, the company evaluates you and your competition, gathering feedback from everyone who interviews you. To be the candidate offered the job, you need to make a lasting impression from the very beginning.

Start by gaining a deep understanding of the position beyond what's in the job ad. Knowing what makes an ideal hire for the role will help you stand out. Reach out to your professional network for insights on the personality traits and skills that are successful in the position. Additionally, research the company, department, and interviewer to get a better sense of what they are looking for in a candidate.

During the interview, try to establish a personal connection with the interviewer. If you have any similarities with them, such as a shared background or interest, use that to your advantage. Be natural and relatable, and don't forget to use their name when speaking or sending an email. Take note of the names of those you meet and refer to them in the future.

Remember, your dream job is also someone else's dream. To stand out, you must do the small things that create a positive memory of your interactions with the company and its employees.

Here are a few things that will help you stand out.

Be fully prepared.

Before your interview, it is crucial to do your research on the company, its history, strategy, and executives. Take note of any information you can gather about the individuals who will be conducting your interviews. This pre-interview preparation will have a significant impact on the actual interview, and will help you establish a connection with the interviewer. The more you know about the company, the more comfortable you will feel answering their questions and the more insightful your questions will be. Use this knowledge to your advantage during the interview and show the interviewer that you are invested in the company and the position.

Keep in mind that your interview will begin as soon as you arrive at the organization.

During job interviews, many companies request feedback from their front desk staff on the applicant's attitude. To present yourself as organized and professional, make sure you have the name of your interviewer and the time of your appointment. Practice polite and professional behavior, including your tone and body language. Remember that as soon as you step inside the building, you are in interview mode and should conduct yourself accordingly.

Unique Value Proposition (UVP).

Crafting a UVP is a powerful tool to establish your personal candidate brand during an interview. It is a concise version of your response to the "Tell me about yourself" question, highlighting your top skills and attributes that overlap with the ideal profile. Your statement should be no longer than thirty seconds, or three to four sentences. This statement can serve as an introduction at job fairs or networking events, or as a way to start a conversation during an interview. You can also use it to support your other answers by providing examples of your skills. For more guidance on crafting an effective UVP statement, refer to the companion workbook.

Be a good listener and answer the questions asked of you.

It may seem obvious, but many candidates start formulating their answer before the interviewer has finished asking the question. This can cause them to miss important details and leave out parts of their answer, giving the impression that they are not good listeners. If you don't listen carefully during the interview, the employer may assume that you will not follow directions or take feedback well on the job. Therefore, it is important to listen carefully to each question and make sure that you fully understand it before providing an answer.

Answer/Ask.

The majority of interviews are structured in a one-sided way where the interviewer asks the questions, and the candidate responds. However, the most impressive candidates are not only able to provide answers but also engage in a professional conversation with the interviewer. This Answer/Ask technique was previously mentioned in the chapter on The Dos and Don'ts of Interviewing. While it may require practice, it can be very effective when executed properly. It should not come across as forced or interrupt the interviewer, but rather should be a natural back-and-forth exchange. A follow-up question can be asked about thirty percent of the time after answering a question, which demonstrates confidence and engagement.

Example: If you are a business analyst and are asked about which ERP systems you have worked with at your last job, answer the question, and then ask something about their ERP system; which system do they use, which version, how long have they used it, how does the interviewer like it? Do not let the interview go too far off-course, but a natural back and forth will make you stand out in a positive way.

Forgive yourself if you make a mistake in the process.
Mistakes happen during interviews, but how you react to them can make all the difference. It's an opportunity to demonstrate resilience and composure in the face of adversity. It is essential to focus on the moment and not allow a mistake to ruin the rest of the meeting. Acknowledge the error, but quickly pivot back to the current question as if it were the first. Interviewers will remember how you handle the situation and your ability to recover more

than the mistake itself. This is a chance to show your ability to handle setbacks professionally and with confidence.

Pay attention to the little things.

Small things often make a big impact when it comes to building a positive impression of yourself as a job candidate. Arrive ten to fifteen minutes early for any in-person interview to demonstrate your punctuality and reliability. If you are going to be late, be sure to communicate with the recruiter or hiring manager in advance. Sending thank-you emails or notes after your interviews is also an important detail that many candidates overlook. While these may seem like simple gestures, they can make all the difference in setting you apart from other applicants who do not take the time to do them.

Closing statement.

When ending an interview, it is crucial to leave a lasting impression on the interviewer. Make sure to express gratitude for their time, convey that you enjoyed meeting them, show interest in the next steps of the process, and give a brief summary of what makes you a good fit for the role.

It's essential to be genuine and specific with your answers. Avoid using rehearsed or monotone responses, as this may cause you to fade into the background or be easily forgotten. Additionally, refrain from over-exaggerating your skills and abilities.

Ultimately, what sets a candidate apart is their unique characteristics and attributes that can benefit the manager and the company. By following the advice in this chapter, you can impress the interviewer and showcase the skills and traits that make you stand out from other candidates.

Best Questions That Candidates Ask the Interviewer

As you near the end of your interview, you will likely be asked if you have any questions for the interviewer. This is a crucial opportunity to gain insights into whether the job is a good fit for your goals, showcase your suitability for the position, and refine your understanding of the ideal profile. Failing to ask questions gives the impression that you are not a serious candidate or are simply seeking any job at the moment.

To make a positive impression, you should ask insightful questions of your interviewers. You can incorporate questions throughout the interview using the Answer/Ask technique mentioned earlier. When asked about remaining questions, ask two or three of the most relevant ones. I have listed some of the best questions from candidates that I have heard below. Before your interview, compile a list of the most relevant seven to ten questions you like. This way, you will still have two or three at the end that were left unanswered. You can even save questions on your phone or on a piece of paper and refer to them during the interview.

(Quick note that most companies will be the ones to bring up compensation. DO NOT ask about compensation at the beginning of an interview process, it shows that your priorities are wrong.)

I have broken down the best questions into four categories:

About the interviewer.

"What was your background before being hired here? How has that benefited you?"

"What do you love most about working here?"

"How would you describe your own management style?"

"What do you enjoy doing outside of work?"

"Is this the career path that you envisioned for yourself when you got your start?"

"What do you wish you knew back when you were in my shoes?"

"Why did you decide to work here?"

Company culture.

"How would you describe the company culture here?"

"What type of employee has been most successful here?"

"What about an employee that did not work out here, why didn't they succeed?"

"What are new employees most surprised by in their first few months here?"

"Why do employees love to work here?"

"What type of hires do not last long with your company?"

Interest in being successful with the company.

"What would you need me to focus on in the first month on the job?"

"What additional responsibilities can be gained over time in this role?"

"What has been the biggest challenge for this role?"

"What are the biggest company goals for the next few years, and how does this position affect those goals?"

"What have people who reported to you in the past done to be successful?"

"What would I need to accomplish in the first year in this job for you to view me as a successful hire?"

"What do you want this role to accomplish in the first 90 days?"

"How do you measure success for the person in this role?"

"What advice would you give to the person you hire in order for them to be successful in this role?"

"What have past employees done to become successful in this type of role here?"

"What are the biggest challenges that the company faces, and how can I help in this role?"

"Who is the company's biggest competitor, and what can I do in this role to help beat them?"

"What is the one trait that you have seen in people who have been very successful in this type of role?"

Due diligence.

"How would you explain this job in your own words?"

"What about my background made you choose me for the interview?"

"What does the interview process look like?"

"Why is the position available?"

"How long has this position been open?"

(If it has already been a couple of months or longer, here is a follow-up: *"What seems to be missing from candidates you have interviewed so far?"*)

"What is your timeframe for hiring someone for this position?"

"What do you think the company's biggest accomplishments will be in the next few years?"

Closing for the offer.

"What skills or experience do you wish I had to make myself a better fit for this position?"

"What are the next steps in the process?"

"What can I clarify about my background to show you that I am the best fit for the job?"

"When would you need me to start?"

(Subtle way to get them to picture hiring you)

"Is there anything in my skills or experience that you feel I am lacking compared to what you are looking for?"

When it comes to the interview process, it's essential to remember that the interviewers will discuss their impressions and recommendations about each candidate throughout and at the end of the process. The questions that you ask or don't ask can significantly impact their decision-making. So, it's crucial to take the time to get it right.

Never say that you have no questions when asked. Use the information gained from your conversation to make any necessary changes for your next interview. Remember to be aware of the time and respect any indications that the interview is coming to a close. Avoid asking questions if the interviewer is running late, as this may cause them to become impatient and leave a negative impression about you.

M. L. Miller

Employer Red Flags

Preparing for an interview can help you become a stronger and more confident candidate. But it's important to remember that the interview is not just about demonstrating why you're the best match for the job. You are also evaluating the company to see if it's a good fit for you.

One way to approach interviewing is to compare it to dating. Like people looking for a romantic partner, employers have an ideal profile of what they want in an employee. They are not trying to determine if you're a good or bad person, but if you're a good fit for what they need.

Just like in dating, a one-sided evaluation process isn't ideal. You have your own idea of what you're looking for in a job and it's important to pay attention to any red flags that may arise during the interview process. Don't be fooled by false positive impressions that could lead to a bad or toxic work situation.

By being aware of what you're looking for and paying attention to any warning signs, you can approach the interview process with more confidence and increase your chances of finding a good match for both you and the company.

Here are employer red flags for you to be extremely cautious of.

Asking you illegal interview questions.

The legality of questions that employers are allowed to ask varies by country and state. It is important to research and understand what can and cannot be asked where you and the employer are located. For example, in the United States, questions regarding age, religion, race, national origin, gender, marital status, pregnancy, or disability are not allowed. In some states, questions about current compensation are also prohibited. However, you can be asked if your age meets a legal requirement for the job, if you are authorized to work in the country, and if you can physically perform the job duties.

If you are asked a question that you believe is prohibited, it is not recommended to be confrontational. Try to answer the question without providing protected information. If the interviewer persists or there is a pattern of illegal questions, politely end the interview and leave. Most countries have a government agency to report such incidents if necessary. It is important to pay attention to red flags, as asking illegal questions can indicate what kind of employer they will be.

High employee turnover compared to other companies in the same industry.

While some employers may experience temporary high employee turnover due to changes in management or strategy, it is important to be cautious of those with a history of frequent turnover. Even if the opportunity seems promising on paper, take the time to understand the reasons behind their high turnover rate.

To gather more information, you can research the company on LinkedIn and compare the number of current employees to previous employees. Additionally, look at the length of time current employees have been with the company. If many employees have been there for less than a year, it could indicate rapid expansion or high turnover. It is crucial to thoroughly evaluate any potential employer to avoid finding yourself in a work environment with a history of instability and turnover.

The description of the job in the interview does not match the description in the ad / or is very unclear.

When an employer describes a different job or is unclear about what the position entails during the interview, it could be a classic bait-and-switch tactic. Employers use this tactic when they realize that the job isn't that attractive. If the job description they give you during the interview is different from what was advertised, it's essential to question a few things. If they change the job description once, will they do it again in the future? How bad is the job if they cannot provide a clear description of it?

Negative atmosphere.

Observing the behavior of employees in a company can give you a good idea of the work environment. Pay close attention to the interaction between co-workers, especially if you are on-site for an interview. Take note of how many employees seem to like each other and appear to be happy working together. If the employees, who are the ones that know the company's work culture best, do not seem content or satisfied, then you should consider that it could be you in the near future. So, be attentive to how the employees behave and interact, as it can be an important factor in deciding whether or not to pursue a job opportunity at the company.

Disrespectful of your time.

When interviewing for a job, it is common courtesy for both the interviewer and the interviewee to respect each other's time. However, there are times when a delay or an unforeseen event may cause the interviewer to be late. In such situations, the interviewer should be apologetic and respectful towards the candidate, who had to wait. This is a red flag that should not be ignored. If the interviewer does not respect your time during the interview process, it is unlikely that they will respect you once you become an employee. While there is no need to be impolite, this behavior should warn you about the kind of culture you may be working in if you accept the job.

Compensation does not match expectations.

When it comes to discussing compensation during the interview process, some companies will disclose the range at the beginning, while others will bring it up at the end. It is crucial to do your research beforehand and have a good understanding of the market value for your position, level of experience, and education. If a company appears to have champagne tastes on a beer budget, be cautious, as it may indicate a culture of expecting more from their employees than they are willing to pay for. However, there are exceptions, such as jobs where gaining experience is the greatest value or startups that may offer equity in the company as compensation. Remember to consider all aspects of the compensation package, including benefits and growth opportunities, when evaluating an offer.

They are asking you to complete free work as part of the interview process.

If a company asks you to complete unpaid work that is part of their regular business, it is a big red flag. Many interview processes include steps where you may be asked to complete a hypothetical exercise as an evaluation tool to test your skill level. However, asking candidates to do work for free is unacceptable, and it should be a warning sign. If their culture permits them to exploit job candidates, then how do you think they are going to treat you as an employee?

Negative company reviews.

Before you go in for an interview, make sure to research reviews online and within your professional network from former employees of the company. Keep in mind that disgruntled former employees may have a bias when writing those reviews, so use it more as a guide to things you should question rather than unimpeachable facts. Look for patterns where the same negative comments are made by multiple former employees. These patterns should be red flags, especially if they relate to your main concerns about the job or company.

During your interview process, pay attention to things you see or hear that match what the negative reviews claim. Take the opportunity to ask questions about any concerns you may have in a respectful and professional manner. This will not only help you to better understand the company's culture and practices, but it will also show the interviewer that you are proactive and engaged in the process.

You are asked about how you have dealt with working with difficult people.

If you hear variations of the question 'Can you deal with difficult people?' multiple times during your interview process, it might be a warning sign of a negative or toxic work environment. Although hearing this question once in an interview is not necessarily a red flag, it is still important to ask follow-up questions to gain a better understanding of the role and the people you may be working with. When answering this question, use the Answer/Ask technique to gather more information. If you get a negative answer, be aware that it could be a sign of difficult co-workers. Be cautious of phrases like 'they have high standards,' 'they're a perfectionist,' or 'they take some getting used to.' These statements could be a warning of a challenging work environment.

They gossip about previous employees.

A toxic workplace can cause a lot of problems, so it is important to avoid them. Gossip is one of the most toxic behaviors that can exist in a workplace, and if an interviewer engages in this behavior during an interview, it is a sign that the company has a toxic culture. If they are willing to smear a former employee's reputation to make themselves look better to you, they will likely do the same thing to you in the future. This is a huge red flag, and you should proceed with caution.

Like dating, the interview process is about finding a good match between employer and employee. Confident and likable people tend to do better in both. It is important to confidently present yourself as a good fit for the job, but also evaluate the employer to see if it is a good fit for you. Ignoring red flags during the evaluation stage can lead to regret later on. Keep presenting yourself as a good match, but continue to ask legitimate questions professionally during the interview process. A good employer will see this as a sign that you are serious about a long-term working relationship.

M. L. Miller

What to Expect from Different Interview Processes

Employers adopt diverse interview formats, and candidates may feel bewildered and distracted when they encounter a format that they did not anticipate. To assist you in navigating through these different interview types, I have compiled a list below, providing details on each one. This will help you become familiar with them, instill confidence, and allow you to remain focused on your objective should you ever encounter them.

Interview formats.

1-on-1.

The one-on-one interview is the most familiar type for job seekers. During this interview, you and the interviewer will have a discussion about your background and the opportunity. The majority of the advice in this book can be directly applied to this type of interview.

1-on-1 sequential.

A series of one-on-one interviews constitutes the sequential interviewing process, where you progress to the next round of interviews if you perform well. Most people are familiar with this format, but it is worth noting that these processes usually culminate in a final interview, which may use one of the other interview formats.

Panel.

The panel interview can be an intimidating experience for candidates. This type of interview involves one candidate meeting with two or more interviewers at the same time. Typically, there are between three to five interviewers on a panel. Employers conduct panel interviews to expedite the hiring process, make collaborative hiring decisions based on seeing and hearing the same things, and train new interviewers. To succeed in a panel interview, it is crucial to remain calm and confident, and avoid focusing solely on one interviewer. Instead, make good eye contact with everyone on the panel, spending slightly more time with the interviewer who asked the question. After the interview, all the interviewers will provide feedback on your suitability for the role, so it is essential to create as many advocates on the panel as possible.

Half/full day.

The half/full day of interviewing format is typically reserved for the final stage of an interview process, as it allows multiple stakeholders to participate in the hiring decision. During this type of interview, you will typically meet with your potential manager, peers, human resources representatives, managers from other teams or departments, and the hiring manager's boss. It is essential to maintain your energy and enthusiasm throughout the day, as this format can be long and arduous. Pay attention to staying hydrated and eating or snacking as needed. It is worth noting that I once had a great candidate perform exceptionally well in the morning interviews, only to perform poorly in the afternoon due to a lack of energy. As a result, they were not hired. Therefore, be mindful of your energy level and enthusiasm in each interview to maximize your chances of success.

Informal.

An informal interview is often used for senior positions, such as taking a candidate to lunch or dinner. However, it can also be as simple as having a peer give you a tour of the facility or chatting with you in the lobby. One common mistake that candidates make during informal interviews is letting their guard down and forgetting that they are still being evaluated. It is crucial to remain relaxed yet professional, positive, and focused on demonstrating how you fit the ideal profile for the position. So, while you should strive to be as comfortable as possible during informal interviews, remember that it is still a part of the interview process.

Phone.

While an initial phone screen is typically a part of most interview processes, it can be included at any point along the way. One of the great advantages of conducting an interview over the phone is that the interviewer cannot see you, which allows you to have your notes, resume, job description, and profile in front of you during the interview. It may seem insignificant, but standing and smiling when you speak on the phone can create a more positive impression. Smiling will make your voice project more confidently and warmly. After the call (or video call) ends, take a few moments to jot down notes while the conversation is still fresh in your memory. Record any comments the interviewer made that provide more insight into the job duties, company culture, or any other information that can give you an advantage in future interviews.

Video.

Video interviews are becoming increasingly common and have presented a learning curve for some candidates. These interviews take place over video conferencing platforms such as Zoom, MS Teams, Google Meet, Skype, or similar platforms. I have seen some candidates turn off their cameras and only use audio during the interview. It is crucial to treat a video interview like an in-person meeting by dressing professionally and always keeping your camera turned on unless you have a technical issue. Many video conferencing platforms offer virtual backgrounds, which can be used if your physical background is distracting. I have also experienced interviews where the candidate's camera was placed to the side of their computer screen, making it appear as though they were not making eye contact. Before any video interview, make sure to test your camera and audio, and position the camera in a way that allows you to give the impression of making eye contact with the interviewer.

One-way video application.

Some companies have begun using pre-recorded video answers to screening questions as part of the application process. In addition to the advice that I gave for video interviews, you should uncover the details of the settings for your video application. Some will allow you to record a video as many times as you want before submitting, while others will have a limit. With formats that limit the times that you can record, you can practice your answers using your smartphone before recording in the application itself.

Peer.

Interviews conducted by potential future co-workers can occur in a formal 1-on-1, panel, video, or casual setting. Such interviews provide a unique perspective and offer insights that may not be available through other interview formats. However, these interviews are also riddled with potential pitfalls. Some candidates may feel overly relaxed when speaking with a peer, which may result in giving negative responses or asking inappropriate questions that they would not ask the hiring manager. To succeed in your interview process, it is essential to remember that you are always being interviewed, and the peer will likely be asked about their interaction with you. So, always maintain a professional demeanor, regardless of who you are speaking to during the interview process.

Stress.

If you are interviewing for a job that will require you to deal with stressful situations, then it is a good idea for the employer to find out how you handle yourself under stress. When I have used this technique, I typically change my tone of voice and act more aggressively towards the candidate, but stress interviews can take on different forms. At the very least you should expect to be asked uncomfortable or stressful questions that are meant to emulate the type of stress in this job. The most successful way to prepare for this type of interview is to do enough research to know whether to expect one. Being surprised by these types of interviews increases the chances of failure. If you do recognize that you are being tested on how you handle stress, try to think about the ideal profile they are trying to hire and do what you can to demonstrate how you would respond if hired. When you are researching the company, do a search with the company name and "Stress Interview" to see if this is something you should expect.

Group.

Group interviews involve a group of candidates meeting with one or a few interviewers at once. While I am not a big fan of this type of interview, its primary purpose is to quickly eliminate candidates. The interviewer will gather several candidates and give a presentation about the job opportunity, which may not be the most attractive job available on the market. Candidates not interested in the position will be instructed to leave, and the interviewer will continue with the remaining candidates. There is not much advice I can offer to perform well in this type of interview as it is more about determining whether the job aligns with your interests. However, ensure that you ask questions and comprehend the role. The reason many employers use a group interview format is that numerous candidates have previously declined the job offer. As such, you should question why this is the case and decide accordingly.

The Job Offer

After successfully completing the interview process, you may have an offer of employment coming your way. Although companies typically make verbal offers, most will follow up with a written offer letter. Your offer will likely have an expiration date since employers need to move on to the next candidate if you decline the offer. One week is the standard time frame, and while you can negotiate the deadline, asking for two or more weeks may suggest that the offer is not your top choice.

While most candidates do not negotiate job offers, those who do tend to earn more money. Negotiating the details of a job offer is more successful if you have followed the advice in this book and created a high-value candidate image with the company. The most crucial piece of advice is that you should negotiate your job offer in most cases. Conduct research to increase your chances of success.

Salary is not the only aspect you can negotiate. Depending on the company, you can request better shifts, company equity, education or training reimbursement, more responsibilities to gain experience, and other benefits.

For more information on successful salary negotiation, please read *SoaringME.com Guide to Successful Salary Negotiation*. However, be cautious when seeking other advice, as I have seen poor advice given by unqualified individuals.

When asked about your salary expectations, avoid staying silent as some suggest. Playing negotiation games may work in some limited cases, but it is not always effective. If an employer wants to hire you, they may overlook any concerns they have about your behavior. However, most of the time, playing negotiation games may make you appear untrustworthy or misguided. Instead, prepare to answer the question about your salary expectations professionally and know what a fair and realistic market price is for your services.

If you found this book to be valuable, please remember to leave a rating to let others know.

Visit SoaringME.com or ask your favorite bookstore for our other books to help your career.

About the Author

M.L. Miller was born in Washington state, grew up in Oregon and, having lived in various places around the United States, he is now back living in the Pacific Northwest with his wife, Wilawan.

Having studied Economics/Finance at the University of Hartford in Connecticut, M.L. began a career in recruitment in 1997, working for hundreds of client companies from Fortune 100 large companies to start-ups. During this time, he has conducted somewhere between twenty and thirty thousand job interviews and has hired thousands of employees in a variety of roles from entry-level positions to C-Suite and Board-Level. During his career he managed a corporate recruiting team, increasing their hires by over 33% in under two years. He started Ethical Recruiters, Inc., an executive recruitment firm and later SoaringME, a company that educates candidates on how to be more successful in job interviewing.

Within this framework, M.L. has also published several books related to the subject:

· *SoaringME The Ultimate Guide to Successful Job Searching.*

· *SoaringME The Ultimate Guide to Successful Job Interviewing.*

· *SoaringME COMPANION WORKBOOK The Ultimate Guide to Successful Job Interviewing.*

· *SoaringME.com: Guide to Successful Salary Negotiation.*

He also has several Ultimate Guides on interviewing for specific careers.

In his free time, M.L. is an avid cyclist and has ridden the annual 200-mile Seattle-to-Portland bike ride five times so far. He also enjoys traveling domestically and internationally.

M.L. has worked with homeless military veterans for a couple of years through a non-profit organization. He used his experience to help them improve interviewing skills, write resumes, and obtain employment to get back on their feet. He also raises money for children's mental health charities.

In the future, M.L. plans to continue his career in talent acquisition. His personal goal is to one day combine his love of cycling and travel to complete 100-mile bike rides on five different continents.

His favorite quote is "Every strike brings me closer to the next home run..." – Babe Ruth.

www.ingramcontent.com/pod-product-compliance
Lightning Source LLC
Chambersburg PA
CBHW071601210326
41597CB00019B/3352